Celtic Quilts

A New Look for Ancient Designs

Beth Ann Williams

Martingale
& COMPANY

Dedication

To "Grandma" Thelma Baldwin and "Aunt" Ada Temple for helping me find my way.

Acknowledgments

My deepest thanks to:

My husband, John, and our daughters, Caryl and Connor, for their unfailing love, support, and willingness to put our lives on hold during my manic efforts to write this book;

My parents, Carol Brennan King and Dr. James King, for their belief in me; and Sue and J. E. Williams for accepting me into their family;

My sister, Amy Logsdon, for her love, her ear, and her ability to visualize the unseen;

My friends, especially Diane Peffer, Nancy Glazier, Roxann Shier, and Barbara Ford, for their encouragement and long-suffering patience while I became temporarily unavailable for anything frivolous and fun;

Connie Young and Peter Walen for sharing their hearts and their books; Connie also for picking up last-minute purchases at the fabric store and bringing over delicious food when I couldn't face cooking;

Sue Callihan for keeping me physically functional; and both Sue and Michael Callihan for their affection and the inspiration I receive when they share their wonderful paintings;

Lori Verbrugge, Pam Crans, and all the ladies of the Grand Quilt Company for their endless generosity, helpfulness, and warm spirits;

All my students for their enthusiasm, dedication, and willingness to be open to new ideas;

The Lord for using even some of the most painful and difficult developments in life to bring joy to the heart.

Library of Congress Cataloging-in-Publication Data
Williams, Beth Ann.
   Celtic quilts: a new look for ancient designs/
Beth Ann Williams.
     p. cm.
   ISBN 1-56477-310-8
     1. Quilting—Patterns. 2. Patchwork—Patterns.
     3. Decoration and ornament, Celtic. I. Title.
TT835.W5347 2000
746.46'089'916—dc21   00-035480

Credits

President . . . . Nancy J. Martin
CEO . . . . Daniel J. Martin
Publisher . . . . Jane Hamada
Editorial Director . . . . Mary V. Green
Design and Production Manager . . . . Stan Green
Project Manager . . . . Tina Cook
Technical Editor . . . . Darra Williamson
Copy Editor . . . . Karen Koll
Proofreader. . . . . Liz McGehee
Cover Designer . . . . Michael Rohani
Text Designer . . . . Kay Green
Illustrator. . . . . Laurel Strand
Photographer. . . . . Brent Kane

Celtic Quilts: A New Look for Ancient Designs
© 2000 Beth Ann Williams
Martingale & Company
20205 144th Avenue NE
Woodinville, WA 98072-8478 USA
www.martingale-pub.com

That Patchwork Place® is an imprint of
Martingale & Company™.
Printed in China
05 04 03 02 01   10 9 8 7 6 5 4

MISSION STATEMENT

We are dedicated to providing quality products and service by working together to inspire creativity and to enrich the lives we touch.

Contents

Introduction

WHO WERE THE CELTS?

The Celts, often called "The Fathers of Europe," became identifiable as a distinct people group around the eighth century B.C.

At one time, Celtic peoples stretched across the face of Europe from Ireland to the Ukraine, and from the Iberian Peninsula (Spain and Portugal) to Asia Minor, rivaling the Roman empire in scope and influence. Although there was never a "Celtic empire," classical Greek and Roman sources recognized individual tribes, such as the Gauls, the Iberians, and the Britons, as sharing commonalities of language, custom, and most importantly for the purposes of this book, material culture.

The Greeks and Romans referred to these various tribes as "Keltoi," or barbarians, a misleading term for today's reader. The Celts (generally pronounced *kelts*) were a highly developed warrior society with rich oral traditions, sophisticated legal structures, and complex personal allegiances based on kinship. They were justly famous for their superb horsemanship and exquisite metalwork.

In their heyday, the Celts enjoyed great military success and renown. In the third and fourth centuries B.C., Celtic tribes sacked Rome, encountered Alexander the Great along the Danube, advanced into Greece, and pillaged Delphi. The Galatians addressed in St. Paul's New Testament epistle were Celts.

However, while the Celts were effective colonizers, they had no centralized authority and were unable to hold their conquests. The Roman invasion of Europe, ending with the conquest of Britain in the first century A.D., sounded the beginning of the end for the Celtic way of life on the European continent. Subsequent invasions of Celtic territories by various Germanic tribes, Vikings, and later the Normans continued the decline, and the Celts were pushed ever westward.

With the spread of Christianity in Ireland in the fifth and sixth centuries A.D., Celtic culture was transformed once again. This time the transition was peaceful, and it lead to arguably the greatest flowering of Celtic art. The spirals, scrolls, compass work, palmettes, foliage, tendrils, triskeles, zigzags, and simple geometric shapes of earlier Celtic cultural periods of Hallstatt and La Tène married with the animal interlace brought by the Germanic invaders of Britain and the stylistic influence of Mediterranean Christianity to produce the style commonly recognized today as "Celtic."

This book focuses on the knotwork and interlace styles associated with this period. However, many of the other above-mentioned Celtic motifs appear in quilts as well.

Traditional Welsh whole-cloth quilts are recognized for their masterful use of spirals, while many quilts in Ireland, the British Isles, and North America have used Celtic-style cables and braids as quilting patterns. Another traditionally favored quilting pattern is the Celtic True Lover's Knot, one version of which appears on page 36.

WHAT DOES "CELTIC" MEAN TODAY?

The influence of Celtic culture continues to the modern day. The term "Celtic Fringe" describes areas perched on the western coast of Europe that still maintain pockets of Celtic culture and—significantly—continue the preservation and/or revival of the old Celtic languages. These areas include Ireland, Scotland, Wales, Brittany, Cornwall, the Isle of Man, and (arguably) Galicia in Spain.

The histories of countries such as the United States, Canada, Australia, and even New Zealand have been profoundly shaped by immigrants with Celtic ancestry.

Celtic art and design continue to be used to support ethnic identity, sometimes coinciding with national political aspirations. They are also often used for the glorification and worship of God, continuing the tradition of the magnificent gospel manuscripts, standing crosses, reliquaries, and liturgical vessels of over a thousand years ago. Others use Celtic symbols to connect with pre-Christian traditions of spirituality.

WHAT IS DIFFERENT ABOUT THIS BOOK?

To me, it is important that Celtic culture be viewed not as a "dead" thing to be studied, dissected, and preserved only in museums and folk parks, but as a living, vibrant expression of honoring our heritage and embracing our future.

The Celts were noted for their love of decoration and for the way they incorporated design and pattern into everyday life, lavishing detail on not only sacred or ceremonial objects, but on functional, everyday items as well. Beauty in form appears to be just as highly valued as efficiency in function. I would like to think that art and design can continue to enrich our lives immeasurably, and that there need not be rigid distinction between art and craft. The one can meld seamlessly into the other.

With this in mind, you'll find that some of the designs in this book are adapted directly from ancient sources, others are modern interpretations of Celtic forms, and still others are brand new designs rooted in Celtic style.

In my original Celtic-style patterns, as well as in my interpretations of historical designs, I have remained true to three characteristics of "classic" Celtic knotwork and interlace:

※ All lines are continuous, having neither beginning nor end.

※ All lines cross each other in an alternating under-over-under pattern.

※ No more than two lines cross at any given point.

The methods used in this book combine traditional techniques with new innovations such as "basting" with pressure-sensitive adhesive, using nylon monofilament thread to machine appliqué with "invisible" stitches, and machine quilting with various decorative threads to add additional texture and interest.

In addition to being innovative, the techniques in this book are *practical*. They are as timesaving and streamlined as possible, and therefore should be accessible to people who may not have huge blocks of time to invest, but still wish to produce high-quality results.

HOW CAN I GET THE MOST OUT OF THIS BOOK?

Begin by carefully reading "Basic Steps in Creating Celtic-Style Appliqué" (pages 11–35). This is the heart of the book, and you will be referred back to this section for every project you choose to make. Review "Equipment and Supplies" (pages 6–10), as well as the supplies listed for each individual project.

If you have never attempted Celtic-style appliqué before, I strongly suggest that you start with a small project, such as "True Lover's Knot" (page 36). You'll appreciate the opportunity to get comfortable with a project that is easy to handle before tackling something more ambitious!

Finally, recognize that although my design sources may be ancient, most of my methods are anything but traditional. As I wrote this book, I shared with you what works well for me and tried to answer questions that may occur to you along the way. I am constantly learning new things, and I'm sure you are too, so if you find a method that works better than mine, go for it! And, while you're at it, maybe you could drop me a line . . .

Equipment and Supplies

FABRIC

Good-quality, colorfast, 100 percent–cotton fabric is the best choice for these projects. It adheres well with the various fusibles and adhesives, holds its shape when pressed, washes easily, and ages gracefully. With the exception of black, I almost never use solid-color fabrics. I find fabrics with visual texture to be much more interesting! An added advantage is that print fabrics tend to help camouflage machine stitching that is supposed to be "invisible."

Wash the fabrics before you use them in order to remove any sizing, finishes, or excess dye. Be particularly careful with reds and purples, as they are the most likely to bleed. (I have rarely had a problem, but when there is one, it can be huge, so it pays to be careful!) Press, if necessary, to remove any wrinkles.

Don't feel that you need to copy the colors and/or prints that I have used: use colors and fabrics *you* like! Just be sure that there is enough contrast between the appliqué fabrics (both bias tubes and insets) and the background fabrics to allow you to see the design clearly.

SEWING MACHINE AND ATTACHMENTS

Sewing machine: It is not necessary to have a fancy or enormously expensive sewing machine for these techniques. All that is required is a good straight stitch and the capacity for a small zigzag stitch. In my experience in the classroom, even the older "no-frills" machines almost always have a stitch setting that is more than satisfactory. That said, however, it *is* true that some machines have features and/or attachments that make the process easier! The bottom line, however, is that you must diligently maintain whatever sewing machine you have, keeping it oiled and cleaning it regularly. Lint and debris can build up quickly, especially in the tension discs, around the presser bar and needle bar, under the needle plate, and around the bobbin area. Your machine will be getting quite a workout, so treat it kindly!

You will also want to know how to change the presser feet, vary stitch length and width, increase or decrease the tension setting for the top thread, raise and lower (or cover) the feed dogs, and adjust the pressure on the presser foot. Depending on your machine, you may also need to change back and forth between a straight-stitch needle plate and a zigzag needle plate. In other words, it may be time to drag that manual out, folks!

Edgestitch/topstitch/blind hem foot: This foot is known by several different names, depending on the manufacturer. It allows you to feed the fabric next to an adjustable guide, simplifying the task of keeping consistent, narrow seam allowances. If this foot is

not available, you can use the straight-stitch foot that came with your machine. This will be discussed in more detail later.

Open-toe appliqué foot: This foot has a large opening in front of the needle, which allows for better visibility while you are stitching. It also has a groove on the bottom, which allows stitches to pass easily underneath. A satin-stitch foot or a zigzag foot is an acceptable substitute, although visibility generally will not be as good.

Walking foot/even-feed foot/plaid matcher: This is another attachment that comes under a variety of guises. Not only is it called by several different names, but its appearance can vary widely as well.

What makes a walking foot unique is that it allows multiple layers of fabric (for example, an entire quilt "sandwich") to move through the machine at an even rate, minimizing shifting. It 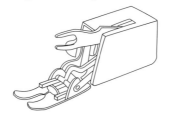 does this by reproducing the action of the feed dogs below on the *top* layer (or layers) of fabric. This foot is indispensable for machine-guided machine quilting, and helpful—though optional—for appliqué as well.

If possible, use the walking foot made especially for your machine. If you cannot find your brand, try a generic walking foot. There are several different styles of generic walking feet; you may have to try more than one before you find a happy fit. Make sure that the *feeders* (also called *teeth* or *grippers*) inside the foot align exactly with the feed dogs on your sewing machine. If they do not, the fabric will not feed evenly, and you may be worse off than if you had no walking foot at all!

Darning/free-motion/spring embroidery foot: Yet another foot that not only goes by a variety of names, but can vary quite dramatically in appearance from one brand to another. This special foot gives you the ability to move the fabric freely from side to side and front to back as you sew. The foot

itself moves up and down with the needle. When the needle is up, you can steer the fabric in any direction. When the needle is down, the foot descends to hold the fabric firmly against the machine's throat plate so that you do not end up with skipped stitches. This foot is indispensable for free-motion machine quilting.

As with the walking foot, it is best to use a foot made especially for your machine. If you cannot find your brand, there are several different styles of generic darning feet. You may need to try more than one.

NOTE: *The feed dogs of your sewing machine must be lowered or covered when you use a darning foot, and the pressure on your presser foot (if adjustable) should be set at 0.*

Sewing-Machine Needles

There are several specialty needles available that make your sewing life much easier and help ensure high-quality results. Needles are grouped by size. European needles are sized based on the measurement of the shaft in hundredths of a millimeter, from 60 to 120. American needles are sized from 8 to 21. The equivalencies are as follows: 60 (European)/8 (American), 65/9, 70/10, 75/11, 80/12, 90/14, 100/16, 110/18, and 120/20.

Needles are also grouped according to type of point. In the descriptions that follow, I have listed the sizes and types of needles I find most helpful for the techniques in this book. I use the Schmetz versions of these sewing-machine needles, but there are other brands available, and you may wish to experiment to find your personal favorites.

Fresh needles are important! Please don't wait until your needle breaks before you change it. Tufts of batting poking through the quilt, skipped stitches, or an odd popping sound when the needle hits the fabric are all signs that it is time for a change.

Microtex Sharps: These needles have a very sharp point and narrow eye. I like to use size 60 or 70 for single-surface machine appliqué (page 21), since the needle makes such a lovely, small hole. Be warned, however, that the size 60 needle can be fragile! A 70/10 jeans/denim needle makes a reasonable alternative.

Quilting needles: These needles were developed specifically for piecing and quilting and have a sharp, tapered point. Size 75 is useful for machine quilting or for appliqué and quilting in one step, especially if you find that your Microtex needles are breaking from the strain of penetrating multiple layers.

Embroidery needles: These needles were designed to handle machine embroidery and decorative stitching. The eye is large and the scarf modified to reduce friction on threads that otherwise have a tendency to fray or split. I like to use sizes 75 or 90 for decorative stitching or machine quilting with rayon threads, with the size depending on the weight of the thread.

THREAD

For appliqué stitching, you will need size .004 nylon monofilament thread, in either clear (for light fabrics) or smoke (for dark fabrics). You'll be pleased to discover that the newer nylon threads are very fine, soft, and stretchy—nothing like the old "invisible" thread.

For quilting by machine, you can choose from nylon monofilament, mercerized cotton, or rayon. Each has its own particular advantages. Nylon monofilament thread sinks into the batting, especially after the quilt is washed, to give texture without adding color. Mercerized cotton is treated for additional sheen as well as strength, so it adds subtle glow along with color. Rayon adds rich color too, with the variegated types adding even more interest by creating highlights as the values change. You can also use metallic thread, but it requires specific techniques that I cannot cover in the scope of this book. Refer to *Machine Quilting with Decorative Threads* by Maurine Noble and Elizabeth Hendricks (That Patchwork Place, 1998) for detailed instructions for working with metallic threads.

Check the edge or bottom of the spool to find the thread weight. I most often use size .004 nylon monofilament; 50-weight, 3-ply mercerized cotton; 60-weight, 2-ply mercerized cotton; or 40-weight rayon, often in variegated colors. *Do not* use nylon monofilament or rayon thread in your bobbin. I normally use 50- or 60-weight mercerized cotton in the bobbin with all of the threads listed above, choosing a color (or colors) that blends with the appliqué and/or backing fabric.

ROTARY-CUTTING EQUIPMENT

Rotary cutter: A rotary cutter with a *sharp blade* makes all the difference when cutting bias strips. Replace your blade often, and you will be amazed at how much easier it is to use!

Cutting mat: You will need a gridded cutting mat at least 24" x 36" (the printed grid may be 23" x 35") in size. These mats can be expensive, but they go on sale pretty regularly. Ask at your local sewing or quilting store, or check the many catalogs that cater to quilters.

Acrylic ruler: Your rotary ruler should be at least 24" long; a 6" x 24" ruler is ideal. Make sure that the lines on your ruler and the grid lines on your mat line up exactly, as sometimes there are slight variations between brands. You'll need a 45-degree line marked on the ruler, as well as clear markings down to ⅛". My favorite rulers have both black and yellow markings, making them easily visible on both light and dark fabrics.

FUSIBLES AND ADHESIVES

Prewash fabric to remove any sizing or chemical finishes before using any fusible product. Do not use fabric softener when you dry the fabric, or starch when you press it, as this may interfere with the bonding process. Read all manufacturer's instructions carefully for the products you have chosen. Use the lowest iron setting that will bond the fabrics successfully. Overheating the adhesive can be just as detrimental as using too little heat.

Steam-A-Seam2: This is a pressure-sensitive adhesive that allows you to temporarily reposition fabrics until you are happy with the results, then iron them in place for a permanent bond. This preliminary bonding and fusing replaces the awkward and time-consuming thread- or pin-basting typical of more traditional appliqué methods.

Quarter-inch-wide Steam-A-Seam2, which comes on a 40-yard roll, is perfect for "basting" bias tubes. You can also buy 12"-wide Steam-A-Seam2 by the yard, which I recommend for inset fabrics. Both varieties have three layers: a layer of adhesive, which looks a bit like rubbery netting, sandwiched between two layers of paper.

If necessary, you may substitute ¼"-wide HeatnBond, The Quilter's Edge Lite for the ¼"-wide Steam-A-Seam2. Other fusible webs, such as Wonder-Under, can be substituted for Steam-A-Seam2 by the yard, although they would be my second choice.

HeatnBond, The Quilter's Edge Lite: This ¼"-wide fusible adhesive can be used in place of ¼"-wide Steam-A-Seam2. This adhesive may be ironed onto the fabric tube, the paper removed, and the tube ironed into place on the background fabric for a permanent bond.

Quick-Bias: Quick-Bias is another product that has become popular recently. It is ¼"-wide, prefolded, preshrunk, iron-on bias tape. After it has been stitched down, it is completely washable. It comes in a variety of colors, and is available by the 5½-yard or 11-yard roll. I buy the 11-yard rolls of black 100 percent cotton for stained-glass-style projects. It can be a bit expensive, but it saves so much in time and labor that I feel it is well worth the price.

Quilt basting spray: Although spray adhesives have been around a while, sprays developed specifically for quilters are fairly new. Select a brand that is easy to use, acid free and ozone friendly, allows for repositioning, and washes free of chemicals when you launder the quilt. Although advertised for use by both hand and machine quilters, I hesitate to recommend it for hand quilting due to the residue that may build up on your needle and the temporary stiffness the adhesive creates in the quilt sandwich. This stiffness washes out when the finished project is laundered.

For small projects, I use basting spray in place of safety pins to hold the layers together for machine quilting. For larger projects, I tend to augment the spray with pins.

Spray adhesive: Acid-free, archival-quality *permanent* spray adhesives, such as those sold for mounting photographs or making art collages, can be used to bond insets in place, although they tend to be somewhat messy. They are not to be confused with quilt basting spray, which is a *nonpermanent* adhesive.

PRESSING ESSENTIALS

Iron: A good, clean iron is essential. Steam is not required for most of the pressing involved in these techniques, although it is helpful for blocking finished quilt projects.

Ironing surface: A pressing surface larger than the typical ironing board is extremely helpful. Try a Teflon-backed pressing blanket, or improvise by layering cotton flannel sheets and/or old cotton towels over thick corrugated cardboard. (The latter protects your table from heat and/or steam damage.)

ASSORTED NOTIONS

Marking tools: Mechanical and chalk pencils, washable graphite markers, and soapstone markers are all useful for marking appliqué designs, inset pieces, and quilting lines. Fine-line permanent pens are important for signing and dating your quilts.

A word of warning: usually it is best to avoid using "vanishing" (purple) and water-soluble (blue) markers for the techniques described in this book. Markings from air-erasable markers often disappear before you are finished working, while ink from water-soluble markers can bleed into the background fabric and become heat-set when pressed during construction of the quilt top, especially if you press with steam.

Bias press bars: These handy tools are available in metal, rigid plastic, and flexible nylon and are sold under several different trade names. I have been most pleased with the plastic variety, but you can use whichever ones you prefer. Widths vary from ⅛" to ¾". For the projects in this book, you will need the ⅜"-wide and the ¼"-wide bars.

Scissors/thread snips: You will need paper scissors for cutting inset shapes from Steam-A-Seam2 and sharp fabric scissors for cutting insets from the actual fabrics. Thread snips or other small scissors are handy to have at your sewing machine for clipping threads as you work. The small size also makes it easy to clip the loops that form when you "jump" intersections during the appliqué process (see page 23).

Seam ripper: A seam ripper does double duty as a stiletto, which is very helpful for holding down the occasional unruly point that wants to come unfolded as you stitch.

Straight pins: I prefer long, fine, flower-headed pins that you can press without melting or leaving marks on the fabric. A very fine shaft is particularly helpful when pinning tightly woven fabrics such as batiks, as pins with thicker shafts can sometimes leave holes.

Safety pins: I recommend medium-size (1½") safety pins to pin-baste the quilt sandwich for machine quilting. Be sure to use pins that are sharp and penetrate the fabric easily. Never use old pins that show signs of rust or other residue, as these can leave permanent stains on your quilt.

Tracing paper: Only the smallest designs will fit on standard 8½" x 11" tracing paper. Sixteen-inch graph paper, designed especially for quilters, is available in many quilt shops and works very well for designs up to 16" in diameter. Another alternative is freezer paper, which comes on 18"-wide rolls and can be found at most large grocery stores in the United States. For larger designs, I particularly like the easel pads that are printed with a very light 1" grid and sold in office-supply stores.

BATTING

I find that low-loft batting is key when working with these patterns and techniques. My preference is for a low-loft 80/20 cotton-poly blend, but I also occasionally use good-quality, low-loft polyester that has been bonded or needlepunched to prevent bearding. Read the package to determine if a particular batting should be washed before it is used and to find out how densely it must be quilted. Compare for yourself, and use what you like!

Basic Steps in Creating Celtic-Style Appliqué

CHOOSING AND ANALYZING THE DESIGN

You can model your projects after the examples I present in the project section of this book, or you can use these examples as a starting point. As you become more experienced in working with this type of design, you may wish to vary size, color, number of insets, and types of borders to make the designs your own. Feel free to interpret the designs for yourself. In other words, experiment and play!

The appliqué designs are composed of fabric strips that are cut on the bias and then stitched to create tubes. You'll need to determine how many *strands*, or *lines*, are included in your chosen appliqué design. Is the design formed of one continuous line, weaving in, out, over, under, and around itself? Or is it composed of completely separate, multiple lines, intertwined with each other?

Design composed of one continuous line

Design composed of two continuous lines

You'll also need to decide what color (or colors) you wish to use for the lines of the appliquéd design. You can use the same fabric for an entire line. Or you can introduce a new fabric at any time, as long as you place it in an "under" position, that is, at a point where the raw edges of the new line are covered by an overlapping line.

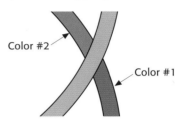

Color #2
Color #1

Insets are the shapes within the pattern lines that are filled with contrasting fabric. Do you wish to use insets to emphasize any of the shapes outlined by the pattern lines? You can use the insets I have suggested in each project, or you can add or omit insets as you prefer, as long as all raw edges of your insets are ultimately covered with a bias tube.

NOTE: *When working on a stained-glass-style design such as "Stained Glass Pillow" (page 52), the bias strips—usually black—act as the "lead," while the colored insets are the "glass."*

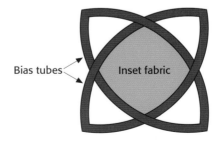

Bias tubes   Inset fabric

You may find it helpful to make a photocopy of the appliqué design you wish to use. Reduce it in size to fit a standard-size sheet of paper, and use colored pencils to audition a variety of color placements. You will be amazed! Sometimes you can achieve startlingly different effects with the exact same design, as demonstrated in the following three quilts:

The first example is the small quilt "Thinking of Danyelle" (page 40). Insets are used to suggest a flower in the center. Tube colors are repeated according to their location within the design, and color does not flow continuously along any of the three lines. The darkest color (purple) is used to create movement by directing your eye outward in a spiral motion.

"Afro-Celt" (page 44), the second example, was influenced by the years I spent living in Africa. Vibrant colors dance on a high-contrast background, and the complementary colors create a pulsing rhythm. There are no insets. The interwoven lines themselves are the dominant feature. Each line is completed in a single fabric.

The final example, "Stained Glass Window" (page 48), gives the illusion of stained glass. Insets have been used for *all* the shapes within the design, and the same ¼"-wide black Quick-Bias has been used for all three lines. In this design, the lines serve only as the setting for the color-rich shapes contained within them.

PREPARING THE BACKGROUND FABRIC

Follow these steps to set guide marks to help you center your design on the background fabric:

1. Fold the background fabric in half horizontally and press with a dry iron.
2. Unfold, then refold the fabric vertically and press again.
3. Once again, unfold the fabric. The point at which the folds intersect marks the center of the background fabric and corresponds to the center of each pattern. Use these folds to guide you in positioning the design on the background fabric.

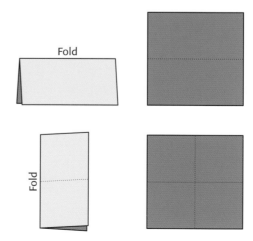

Transferring the Pattern to Fabric

I prefer to trace my pattern onto a sheet of paper first to ensure that the "over" and "under" lines are accurately positioned. Then I am ready to transfer the design to the background fabric.

TIP

You may wish to take your book to a copy or print shop and have it spiral bound. In my area, this generally costs about two or three dollars. It is much easier to trace the pattern sections from a spiral-bound book, since the pages lie nice and flat.

1. Choose an appropriate marking tool (see "Marking Tools" on page 9). In most cases, a simple mechanical pencil works best. If you are using a very dark background fabric, a chalk pencil will do the job nicely.

2. Position and tape the prefolded background fabric and pattern onto a light table or other tracing surface. Be sure to use masking tape, which won't leave sticky residue on the glass.

   A light table is a definite plus when tracing patterns, but if you do not have one, don't despair! You can improvise by placing a lamp under a glass table or an open table with the leaves removed. Just set a sheet of glass in the opening. Another alternative is to tape the pattern to a sunny window.

   I prefer a large tracing surface that I can use, then put away. My solution is a 3' x 4' sheet of heavy glass with taped edges. This glass sheet is raised and supported by the clear plastic shoebox containers I use to sort fabric strips. (I originally used big cans of pie filling!) I position a 16" flourescent light beneath the glass. Although the lamp is the type you can mount permanently, I keep it portable so that I can move it around to illuminate the part of the design I need to trace.

TIP

Plexiglas makes a good alternative to glass in an improvised light table. It is lighter and probably safer, too!

3. Check to make sure that the center of the pattern is lined up with the intersection of the pressed folds in the background fabric and trace.

4. If the design is fairly simple, you may choose to trace a single line down the center of the pattern's double lines. This reduces tracing time. For more complex patterns, however, you'll find it best to trace both lines exactly as they appear in the printed patterns, since it becomes more difficult to keep track of overlaps, intersections, and exact line placement with only a single line to guide you. Be sure that the double-traced lines are narrower than the bias tubes you plan to use, so that they are covered when the appliqué is sewn in place.

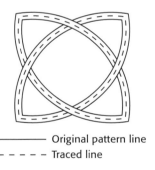

——— Original pattern line
- - - - - Traced line

Placing the Fabric Insets

There is no need to turn under the edges of inset shapes. The raw edges will be "finished" when they are covered by the bias tubes.

Insets must be applied before the bias tubes are stitched in place. Remember these hints when preparing and placing insets:

Add generous seam allowances when cutting the inset shapes. For example, when working with ⅜" finished bias tubes, I add a full ¼" seam allowance to the insets. This greatly reduces the likelihood that the raw edges of the insets will creep out from underneath the bias tubes when the finished quilt is used and laundered.

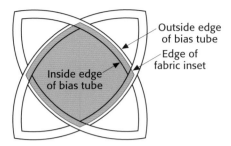

Overlap inset shapes if necessary as you place them on the background fabric. Generally, I place the outermost shapes first and work my way toward the center, which becomes the final piece.

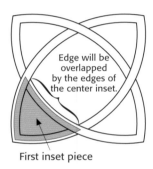

Personally, I find that bonding insets provides the greatest security over time and handling, and prefer to use 12"-wide Steam-A-Seam2, as it is the most "forgiving" fusible. If you make a mistake or simply change your mind about a particular fabric, it is easy to remove or reposition the offending piece without destroying your work. And since inset shapes can be traced directly from the pattern onto the fusible product, no inset templates are required.

To use Steam-A-Seam2 for inset shapes:
1. Preheat a steam iron to the cotton setting.
2. Trace the inset shape onto the Steam-A-Seam2. Trace onto the side where the paper is most loosely attached to the adhesive.
3. Cut out the shape with paper scissors. Don't forget to add a seam allowance!
4. Remove the layer of paper on which you traced the inset shape.
5. Stick the inset shape, adhesive side down, firmly onto the wrong side of the inset fabric.

6. Carefully cut around the shape (including seam allowance) with fabric scissors.
7. Remove the remaining layer of paper.
8. Stick the shape into place on the background fabric.
9. Pieces may be repositioned as desired. When final placement is determined, press for 5 to 10 seconds with the preheated iron. The pieces will be permanently bonded.

If you prefer, you may use an acid-free, archival-quality spray permanent adhesive (*not* basting spray; see page 9) to adhere the insets to the background fabric:
1. Trace the inset shape onto the paper (non-waxy) side of a sheet of freezer paper, adding seam allowances.
2. Cut the shape out of the freezer paper and press it, waxy side down, onto the right side of the inset fabric. The wax will soften, adhering the freezer paper to the fabric.
3. Cut the shape out of the fabric, right along the edge of the freezer paper. Leave the freezer paper in place.
4. Working on a covered surface in a well-ventilated area, spray an even coat of adhesive onto the backside of the inset shape. I generally spray several pieces at a time.
5. Use your fingers to press the inset shape into place on the background fabric.
6. Remove the freezer paper from the front of the inset shape.

PREPARING THE BIAS TUBES

It is vital to use strips cut on the bias to construct the fabric tubes required for the appliqué designs in this book. Strips cut on the lengthwise or crosswise grain of the fabric will pucker and bunch since they do not have the stretch and flexibility needed to go around curves.

You may find yourself with a bit of

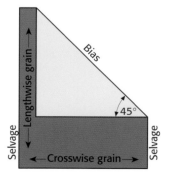

leftover fabric when cutting bias strips, but it is important to start with a piece of fabric that is at least 16" to 18" wide after washing and pressing. Otherwise, the cut strips will be short and awkward to use. For the projects in this book, I suggest you work with fat quarters or ½-yard cuts of 42"- to 44"-wide fabric. Fat quarters are simply ½-yard pieces of fabric that have been cut in half horizontally, resulting in two ¼-yard pieces that measure approximately 18" x 22", rather than the standard 9" x 44".

First, you'll need to determine the desired finished width of the tubes required for your project. Generally speaking, I find ⅜"-wide bias tubes the most pleasing to use for most projects, and you will find that most of the projects in this book call for tubes of this width. The ⅜"-wide tubes are wide enough to handle easily, yet not so wide as to become cumbersome. I also like the way the ⅜" width *looks* on the finished quilt. It has more visual "weight" than a narrower width and allows the colors used in the bias tubes to show up more clearly. In most cases, you will need to cut 1"-wide strips for tubes that measure ⅜" wide. Exceptions are noted in "Sewing the Bias Tubes" on page 16.

Next, you'll want to estimate the total number of strips you will need to cut for the project. There are two ways to do this. You can lay string or yarn along all the lines of the pattern, measure the length needed, and add an extra 10" to 20" for insurance, depending on the size of the design. Or, you can lay the actual strips over the design as you cut them, overlapping the pointed ends and making sure that all strips end in the "under" position.

There is no advantage to joining the strips into long lengths or cutting continuous bias from a large tube. It is actually easier to work with the strips in the lengths yielded by the bias of a fat quarter or ½-yard piece. All but the shortest strips (e.g., those with a finished length less than 6") usually work.

Cutting the Bias Strips

You'll need a rotary cutter, a large cutting mat, and a rotary ruler at least 24" long to cut the bias strips required for these projects (see "Rotary-Cutting Equipment" on page 8).

1. Position the fabric on the gridded side of your cutting mat so that the lengthwise and crosswise straight of grain aligns with the vertical and horizontal grid lines. If you are using a fat quarter or ½-yard cut of fabric, turn it so that the 18" side runs crosswise (horizontally). Check the fabric threads as you align the fabric. You may notice that the edges of the fabric do not end up perfectly straight on your mat, since many of today's fabrics are not woven perfectly on-grain.

   I often layer and cut up to three fabrics at a time. I find that fabric has less tendency to slide around, and the rotary cutter has less tendency to veer away from the ruler, with the added resistance of several layers on my cutting board.

2. Begin cutting approximately 6" from the lower-left corner of the fabric. Align the 45-degree marking on your ruler with the first horizontal grid line visible on the mat below the fabric's bottom edge. Make a cut, creating a "waste" triangle. Set this triangle aside for use in another project.

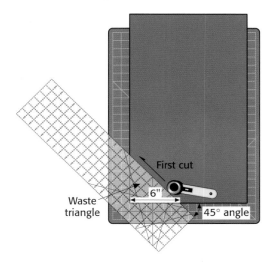

Don't plant your hand on the middle of the ruler and expect to make accurate cuts! Carefully "walk" and reposition your hand up the length of the ruler as you cut. This helps to steady the ruler and prevents it from shifting.

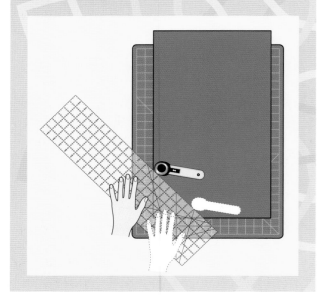

3. Use the appropriate line on your ruler to measure and cut the first strip. Strip width will depend upon the desired finished width of the bias tubes and the foot attachment you use to sew the bias tubes (see "Sewing the Bias Tubes" at right).

4. Continue cutting until you have the number of strips required for your project. Periodically recheck the position of the 45-degree angle marking on your ruler. If necessary, retrim the cut edge of the fabric to "true up" the angle.

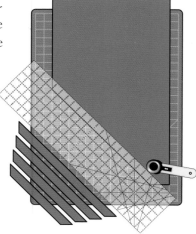

Sewing the Bias Tubes

Methods for sewing the bias tubes vary slightly, depending upon the foot attachment you are using on your sewing machine.

If you are using a topstitching, edgestitching, or blind hem foot:

1. Cut bias strips 1" wide.
2. Set the guide screw on the presser foot to establish a *scant ⅛"-wide* seam allowance. A thread or two under ⅛"-wide will usually do.
3. Fold the cut strips in half, wrong sides together.

1"-wide bias strip
Wrong side
Fold

4. Carefully stitch down the long raw edge, feeding the fabric next to the guide to take a scant ⅛"-wide seam.

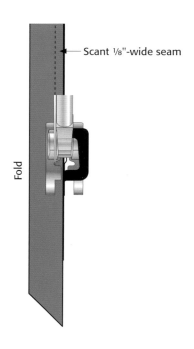

Scant ⅛"-wide seam
Fold

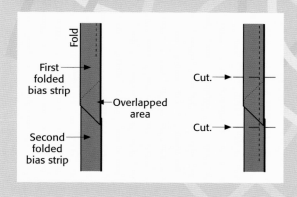

First folded bias strip — Fold

Overlapped area

Second folded bias strip

Cut. Cut.

If you do not have a topstitching, edgestitching, or blind hem foot, or find it difficult to sew a consistent scant ⅛"-wide seam, you may substitute a standard straight-stitch presser foot and follow these steps:

1. Cut bias strips 1¼"wide.
2. Fold the strips in half, wrong sides together.

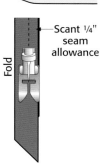

1¼"-wide bias strip

Wrong side

Fold

3. Carefully sew down the long raw edge, taking a *scant* ¼"-wide seam allowance. A thread or two under ¼" will usually do.

Scant ¼" seam allowance

Fold

4. When you are finished sewing the tubes, use your rotary cutter and ruler (or fabric scissors) to trim the seam allowance to a scant ⅛".

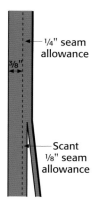

¼" seam allowance

⅜"

Scant ⅛" seam allowance

Pressing the Bias Tubes

Here are two methods for using bias press bars (see page 9) to press bias tubes into nice, crisp lengths for appliqué. Method 2 is my favorite, but experiment to see which method you prefer.

Method 1:

The main drawback to this method is that even plastic bars can get very hot, so you'll need to take care to avoid burned fingers!

1. Slide the fabric tube onto the bias press bar of the appropriate width, that is, the widest bar that fits comfortably. For most of the projects in this book, this will be the ⅜"-wide bias press bar. Center the seam allowance—if necessary, trimmed to ⅛"—on the back of the bar.

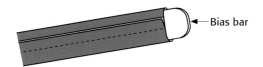

Bias bar

2. Press the tube, turning the seam allowance to one side.

3. For longer strips, continue sliding the bar inside the tube and pressing, until the full length of the tube has been pressed flat. Carefully remove the tube. Depending upon the bar you are using (metal, plastic, or nylon), you may need to give the tube an additional press after the bar is removed.

Method 2:

1. Slide the fabric tube onto the bias press bar of the appropriate width as in Method 1, step 1. But this time, scrunch the tube up at one end of the bar, keeping the seam allowance centered on the back side of the bar.

Bias bar

2. Slide the tube, bit by bit, off the bar, pressing small sections at a time. Take care to keep the seam allowance centered.

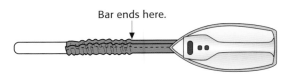

Bar ends here.

Be careful not to stretch the tube as you are feeding it off the bar. If you stretch a tube now, it will lose some of the stretchability it needs to curve smoothly around the curves of your design. Proceed with care!

TIP

You'll find it helpful to have a hard surface for pressing. A standard ironing board cover has just enough "give" to make it difficult to achieve a nice, sharp crease. An empty fabric bolt is ideal, and most quilt shops or fabric stores will be happy to let you have one for free.

"BASTING" THE APPLIQUÉ DESIGN

Using My Favorite Method: Steam-A-Seam2

It is, of course, possible to make Celtic quilt designs without using Steam-A-Seam2 (see page 8). Using it, however, makes life a whole lot easier! I buy the ¼"-wide rolls for minimum-fuss "basting" of bias tubes. Because the adhesive is pressure-sensitive, it sticks to the background fabric when the tube is finger-pressed into place. The bond is not permanent at this point, so wayward tubes can be repositioned, and "over" sections easily lifted to tuck raw edges underneath. Once everything is in place, a permanent bond is achieved by pressing with an iron. This effectively bastes the design for sewing without the nuisance of pins sticking out everywhere, and without the tedium of thread-basting—either stitching it or removing it!

I have generally found this product a joy to use, but no method is 100 percent foolproof. If you should have a problem with the product sticking, make sure that the problem is not caused by any finishes, starch, or fabric softener on the fabric itself. If that is not a factor, and the strips of Steam-A-Seam2 do not adhere to the fabric even when finger-pressed very firmly, it may be time to try a fresh box of Steam-A-Seam2 or move on to an alternative method.

Since the backing tends to separate from Steam-A-Seam2 as it is handled, apply Steam-A-Seam2 to the fabric tubes one at a time, as you use them.

1. Measure out a length of ¼"-wide Steam-A-Seam2 next to the fabric tube that you plan to fuse. Cut the Steam-A-Seam2 to this length.
2. Remove one layer of the paper backing and finger-press *firmly* to adhere the Steam-A-Seam2 strip to the wrong side (seam allowance side) of the fabric tube. Peel off the remaining layer of paper backing.

3. Find a place in the appliqué design where a fabric tube of the color you are holding appears in the "under" position, that is, a place where it will be crossed over (and therefore covered) by another tube. Finger-press the tube onto the background fabric, beginning at the "under" spot, and slightly overlapping the outer placement line for the "over" tube. Continue finger-pressing firmly to position the strip, covering the placement lines marked on the background fabric, until you have overlapped the outer placement line for the *next* "over" tube. Trim the tube if necessary.

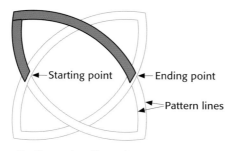

Starting and ending points will be covered by the "over" tube.

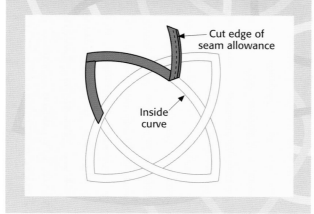

4. Continue adding fabric tubes as described in step 3. Always end your tube in the "under" position, so that all raw edges will be covered by another tube, and overlap these cut ends so that they will not pull out and become exposed when you are laundering your finished project.

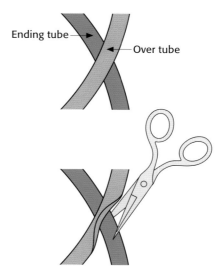

5. When your design is completely finger-pressed in place, follow the directions on the Steam-A-Seam2 package to press it with your iron. The heat melts the adhesive to form a permanent bond between the fabric tubes and the background fabric.

Handling Points

It is one thing to work in fullness for a perfectly mitered point when appliquéing by hand. When using the sewing machine, however, it is quite another matter! Many people have great difficulty making consistently neat machine miters when maneuvering bias tubes under the presser foot. That's why it made sense to me to devise a simpler method for achieving satisfactory results!

1. As you approach a point, finger-press the tube in place all the way up to the point.
2. Fold the tube back over itself, creating a tuck between the layers. To make the turn, reposition the tube so that its starting edge is even with the outer edge of the original tube. Iron and then stitch down the point for a perfectly flat finish.

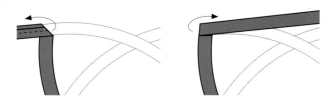

Alternative "Basting" Methods

If Steam-A-Seam2 is not available, or you prefer to try another simplified method of basting, here are a few alternatives you might try.

HeatnBond, The Quilter's Edge Lite

This ¼"-wide, iron-on adhesive comes on a roll. The backing stays on until you peel it off, so you can prepare all the tubes at once.

1. Measure out a length of ¼"-wide HeatnBond next to the fabric tube that you plan to fuse. Cut the adhesive to this length.
2. Iron the adhesive to the wrong side (seam-allowance side) of the fabric tubes.
3. As you get ready to position each tube, peel the paper backing from the adhesive, and iron the tube in place. Begin at an "under" point, and continue as described for "Using Steam-A-Seam2," steps 3 and 4 (see page 19), pressing with an iron instead of your fingers. I find it helpful to work with the iron in one hand and the fabric tube in the other. Guide the tube along the marked design, and follow with the tip of the iron about ½" behind, pressing as you go. Work a small section at a time. Don't worry about what is happening with the rest of the tube; concentrate only on the little section right in front of the iron.

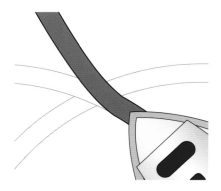

4. Give the entire design a press after it is completed, just to make sure it is securely bonded. Be careful, however, not to overheat the adhesive! It will not bond if it gets *too* hot.

Quick-Bias or Other Purchased Fusible Bias

The advantages: There is no prep work with fabric here. The bias is ready to fuse into place—right off the roll! The black is especially nice for "stained glass" work, and the narrow width keeps the focus on the beautifully colored "glass."

The disadvantages: It can be expensive, and it comes in a somewhat limited range of colors. And, though often suitable for small or detailed motifs, the ¼" width is narrower than I normally prefer for large designs.

Quick-Bias and most other purchased fusible products are not pressure-sensitive like Steam-A-Seam2. Like HeatnBond, they must be bonded with heat. I generally work in the same manner as I do when applying HeatnBond, guiding the fusible bias into position with one hand, while the other hand steers the iron about ½" behind.

APPLIQUÉING THE DESIGN

"Invisible" Appliqué by Machine

This is the method used for all of the quilts in this book. Invisible machine appliqué provides the speed and efficiency of machine work while preserving the heirloom look achieved by hand.

Before you begin, you must make a decision: would you like to appliqué and quilt all in one step (which is generally faster), or would you prefer to complete the appliqué on the quilt top before layering the quilt sandwich (which is generally easier)? The size of the project and your level of machine-quilting experience will probably determine the best choice for you.

If you wish to appliqué and quilt in one step, make a final check of the basted tubes against the master pattern for the correct sequence of "unders" and "overs." Also check to be certain that all raw edges are completely concealed. Refer to "Adding Borders" on page 24 to add any borders as suggested for the pattern you have selected, and then layer and secure the quilt sandwich with the basting method of your choice (see "Basting the Quilt Sandwich" on page 26.)

If you are making multiple blocks, if the project is either complex or more than 30" wide, or if you are simply more comfortable working with a single layer at a time, you will probably wish to appliqué each block separately before assembling the complete quilt top. If that is the case, don't worry about adding borders or basting layers at this time. Rather than quilting and appliquéing in one step, you can work on the quilt top only. This process is called *single-surface appliqué*.

If you are still undecided, I have made recommendations in the instructions for each project to guide you. Either way, you'll need to do a little preparation before beginning to stitch.

Preparing to Stitch

1. Prepare your machine by inserting a new needle. See "Sewing-Machine Needles" on page 7 for suggestions as to which needle to use for your preferred technique.

2. Select suitable thread (see page 8). The color of the background fabric is irrelevant when choosing the thread color for this technique. Instead, you need to consider the color and value (light, medium, or dark) of the appliqué fabrics. If the fabric tubes are medium to dark in value, use smoke-colored nylon monofilament thread. If the tubes are light to medium in value, use clear nylon monofilament thread.

   Remember: do not put monofilament thread in your bobbin! Instead, I recommend either 50- or 60-weight mercerized cotton thread in a color that matches or blends with the bias-tube fabrics. This prevents tiny dots of bobbin thread from showing, particularly as you are perfecting your technique.

3. Take the time to try a few test swatches first, using trimmed bits of bias tube left over from "basting" the appliqué design in place. If you will be appliquéing the quilt top only, use a single piece of fabric as your practice background. If you plan to appliqué and quilt in one step, make yourself a mini quilt sandwich for practice purposes. It is important that you

determine a pleasing and satisfactory stitch size and style before starting on the real thing! The two recommended stitches for machine appliqué are a short blind hem stitch or a narrow, short zigzag. Experiment on your machine to find out which you prefer.

The blind hem stitch takes about three straight stitches along the outside edge of the appliqué shape, then takes a bite into the shape itself.

Blind hem stitch

I prefer to use a small zigzag stitch. I set my machine for a stitch *width* of 1.5. Sometimes I'll drop down to 1.0, but this can be harder to see, and therefore harder to control. I set the stitch *length* at 1.5.

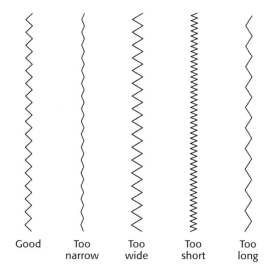

| Good | Too narrow | Too wide | Too short | Too long |

Zigzag stitch

Please note that stitches can vary widely from machine to machine, so you will need to experiment. Use the settings that work best for your particular machine, even if different than what I recommend here. Just be certain that one side of your zigzag stitch catches a few threads of the fabric tube and the other side of the stitch just barely drops off the edge of the tube into the background fabric.

4. Select a comfortable starting point for your stitching. I look for an intersection near a spot in the design that is either fairly straight or *gently* curved. By all means, avoid starting on a point or on a tight curve! When possible, plan to stitch inside curves first, although it is not strictly necessary to do so.

The Stitching Process

Now you are ready to stitch!

1. To avoid a nasty nest of thread on the back side of your work, bring the bobbin thread up through all layers.
    A. With the top thread held above (and free of) the presser foot, lower the presser foot.
    B. Use the hand wheel on your machine to make one complete stitch, with the take-up lever starting *and* stopping in the highest position.
    C. Tug gently on the "tail" of the top thread. A loop of bobbin thread should pop up through all the layers.
    D. Pull the end of the bobbin thread through to the top layer. This allows you to hold both threads under the presser foot and out of the way as you start to stitch.
    E. Continue holding both the top and the bobbin threads until you have locked your stitches (see step 2). You can go back and clip these threads later.
2. Secure your stitches with a *locking stitch* (several stitches almost on top of each other) or with ¼" of very tiny stitches.

3. Stitch down each section of fabric tube. "Jump" over crossovers as shown, making sure to use a locking stitch to secure stitches on either side of the jump. Jumping the intersections will leave a loop of thread on both the front and back sides of your work. You will clip these threads later.

"Jump" here.

TIP

I tend to disregard the "over/under" rule when I use ¼"-wide black Quick-Bias. When sewn down, the "overs" and "unders" are practically invisible, and therefore not worth the trouble! Instead, I sew straight through all intersections.

If you dislike using nylon monofilament thread, you may use 60-weight black mercerized cotton embroidery thread (on top and in the bobbin) to appliqué black Quick-Bias. However, if you happen to stitch into the background, the wayward stitching will be much more visible than if you had used the smoke-colored nylon monofilament.

4. Stitch down the entire design. Be sure to sew both edges of each fabric tube. If you find that you are veering off the edge of the tube, don't panic! Simply reverse your stitching to get back to where you were last "on target," and then start stitching in a forward direction again. One of the advantages of using nylon monofilament thread is that the extra stitching usually doesn't show on the front!

5. Check to make sure that there are no gaps in your stitching.

6. Clip threads at all jump (crossover) points. If you have chosen to appliqué and quilt in one step, you will need to clip the loops on both the top and back side of the quilt sandwich. If you are doing single-surface appliqué (appliquéing on the top layer only), you need only clip the loops on the front side of your work.

TIP

Since tiny clippings of thread—especially nylon monofilament—are so hard to see, I wrap a large loop of tape around my fingers and "pat down" my quilts. The tape collects any bits of thread that may be clinging to the surface of the quilt.

A Word About Hand Appliqué

If you wish, you can hand appliqué any of the projects in this book. My friend Jane Levering was kind enough to demonstrate this by hand appliquéing (and hand quilting) the sample below using the preparative methods I've described so far.

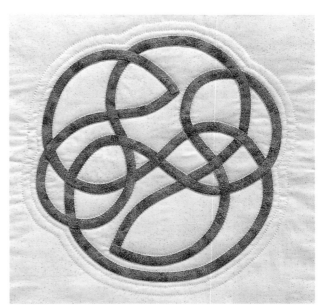

Unfortunately, a complete discussion of hand appliqué is beyond the scope of this book. However, Jane suggests that using 100-weight silk thread is the key to beautifully "invisible" hand stitching. With silk thread, it is not necessary to match thread color to every fabric. Although it is quite strong, silk thread is so fine that it sinks down and virtually disappears into the fabric. As a result, Jane finds that two neutral colors—one very light and one a bit darker in value—are all that she needs for her hand appliqué.

To hand appliqué, bring the needle up through the background fabric, barely catching the edge of the fabric tube. Bring the needle back down, this time through only the background fabric.

Make short, straight stitches.

You may wish to refer to *Basic Quiltmaking Techniques for Hand Appliqué* by Mimi Dietrich (That Patchwork Place, 1998) for complete instructions on hand-appliqué techniques.

ADDING BORDERS
Butted (or Squared) Borders

Unless I am using a striped border fabric that needs to be mitered for design reasons, I prefer to use *butted* (or *squared*) borders. Not only do they save fabric, but they are much easier for most quilters to do well consistently.

Border measurements are given with the specific instructions for each applicable project in this book. Nonetheless, it is always a good idea to measure *your* quilt top and adjust the border measurements as necessary before sewing the border strips to the quilt. Add one border to all four sides of the quilt before adding any subsequent borders.

1. Measure the quilt top through its vertical *center*. (Sometimes the edges or corners of a quilt top can become stretched or splayed, throwing off the measurements.)

This is the "true" measurement for the two side border strips. Make any adjustments that might be necessary to the side border measurements given in the project instructions.

2. Careful pinning prevents the border strip from migrating down the quilt top as you sew, and evenly distributes any excess fullness. Fold each side border strip to find its midpoint. With right sides together and long raw edges aligned, pin the border strips to the left and right sides of the quilt top, matching the borders' midpoints to the midpoints of the quilt top. Next, match and pin the ends; then place additional pins in between to ease as necessary.

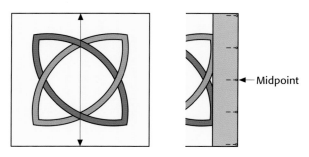

3. Using a ¼"-wide seam, sew the side borders to the quilt top. Press the seam allowances toward the borders, away from the center of the quilt. Always press each seam before adding the next border strip.

4. Measure the quilt top through its horizontal *center* (including the side borders). This is the "true" measurement for the top and bottom border strips. Make any adjustments that might be necessary to the border measurements given in the project instructions. Pin and sew the top and bottom borders to the quilt as directed in steps 2 and 3.

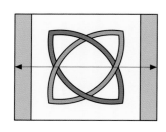
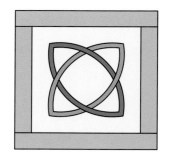

Narrow Accent or "Flap" Borders

Several projects in this book incorporate a narrow border that is actually a flap. In most cases, this flap finishes ⅜" wide and adds an important accent, or flash of color, between the inner and outer borders of the quilt project.

1. Attach the first (inner) border to all four sides of the quilt top as described in "Butted (or Squared) Borders" on page 24. Don't be put off by how wide this initial border seems; some of the width will be covered by the flap.

2. Measure and trim the side flap borders as you did for the side inner borders. Fold the flap borders in half, wrong sides together, matching the long raw edges, and press.

3. Pin the side flap borders to the sides of the quilt top as before, this time aligning the raw edges of the folded flap borders with the raw edges of the inner borders. The folded edges should face the center of the quilt, covering up some of the inner border.

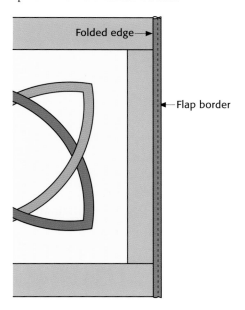

Folded edge →

← Flap border

4. Sew the side flap borders to the quilt, using a *scant* ¼"-wide seam allowance. Press.

5. Repeat to measure, trim, pin, and sew the top and bottom flap borders.

6. Measure, trim, then pin the outer side borders to the quilt top, aligning their raw edges with the raw edges of the two previous borders. Sew the border strips to the quilt, using a ¼"-wide seam allowance. Press the seam allowance toward the outer border, away from the center of the quilt.

Press seam allowance toward the outer border.

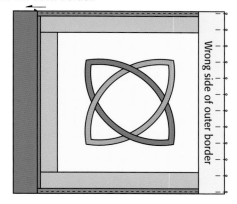

Wrong side of outer border

7. Repeat to measure, trim, pin, sew, and press the outer top and bottom borders.

The flap can be left free, or the folded edge can be appliquéd down with the same stitch used to sew the bias tubes in place. I use both techniques. Sometimes I appliqué the flap down so that it becomes a narrow accent border, as in my quilt "Afro-Celt" (page 44). At other times, as in "Morning Glory" (page 65), I opt to leave the flap free, creating a three-dimensional accent.

"Afro-Celt," detail of flap border. For full view, see page 44.

"Morning Glory," detail of flap border. For full view, see page 65.

BASTING THE QUILT SANDWICH

Unless you are planning to hand quilt your project, I suggest that you do not baste in the traditional sense; that is, hand sew with large stitches. For medium-to-large wall hangings, lap quilts, or bed quilts that will be quilted by machine, I prefer to baste my quilt sandwich with safety pins, usually spaced about 3" apart.

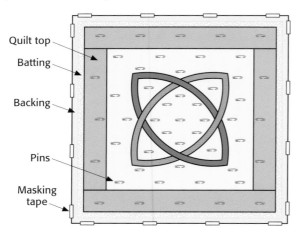

Be sure to cut the batting and backing a few inches larger than the quilt top. A good rule of thumb is to cut the backing fabric at least 3" to 4" larger, and the batting at least 1" to 2" larger than your quilt top on all sides.

Basting with Safety Pins

1. Press both the quilt top and backing to remove any wrinkles.
2. Lay the backing wrong side up on a clean floor or tabletop.
3. Use wide masking or packing tape to tape down all the edges. Begin by taping the midpoints of each side, then the corners. Finally, fill in around the entire perimeter of the quilt as necessary. The backing fabric should be smooth and taut, but not stretched so tightly that the fabric becomes distorted, creating a mess of wrinkles and tucks when the tape is removed.

If you are working on a tabletop, and the surface is smaller than your quilt, you may use clamps or binder clips instead of tape to secure one or more edges of your backing fabric.

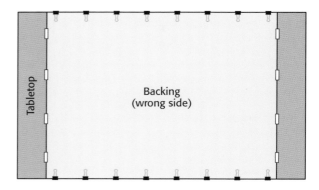

TIP
When taping a quilt back to the floor or table, test the tape first to be sure it will not ruin the surface finish when you remove it.

4. Center the batting, and then place the quilt top right side up on the backing and smooth it in place.
5. Start pinning! Unlike many quilters, I like to pin the outer edges first, so that I don't disturb or distort them when I reach (or crawl) over them to pin the interior of the quilt. However, if you are concerned that you might end up with a center bulge, you can start pinning in the center and work outward.

As soon as the edges of the quilt sandwich have been pinned securely, I start placing pins in the areas in and around the appliquéd designs. Finally, I pin any remaining areas in grid fashion, once again placing pins at about 3" intervals.

6. Unless I need to crawl over some of the safety pins to reach other areas of the quilt, I prefer to wait until the pins are all in place before I start closing them. While some people swear by fancy purchased notions to help close safety pins, I find that my daughter's old baby spoon works just fine for me! Slide the bowl of the spoon under the tip of the pin and hold it steady. Then, with your other hand, press down on the pin to close it.

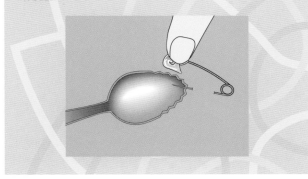

Basting with Basting Spray

For smaller wall hangings, table runners, table mats, and pillow tops that will be quilted by machine, quilt basting spray is a fantastic timesaver. Please note that this is not the same as using photomount or craft adhesive sprays. See the description of basting spray on page 9.

Read all directions on the product can before beginning. It is essential that you work in a well-ventilated area. Be sure to use a plastic drop cloth or suitable alternative to avoid covering your work area with spray.

1. Spread the batting over the covered work surface, smoothing out any wrinkles.
2. Shake the can of spray vigorously and, following the product directions, spray an even coat of adhesive over the entire piece of batting.
3. Center the backing fabric right side up over the sprayed batting. Use your hands to smooth the backing in place from the center outward. If bubbles or wrinkles appear, lift up the backing fabric and reposition it immediately, smoothing as you go.
4. Flip the sandwich over and spray the other side of the batting.
5. Center and smooth the quilt top in place. Push down firmly at this point, just to make sure the layers are well adhered. Recheck both sides for ripples.
6. Fold the excess backing fabric over to the front and finger-press it in place to cover the sticky batting left exposed around the edges of the quilt top.

You can take the quilt sandwich to the sewing machine and begin stitching immediately, but you'll probably find that there is much less residue on the machine's needle if you wait a few hours. An overnight wait is even better.

CHOOSING A QUILTING METHOD

"Quilt as desired." Don't you hate seeing that ambiguous phrase at the end of a great pattern? Read on for some practical suggestions for quilting the projects in this book. Keep in mind that quilting may be done by either hand or machine.

If you have appliquéd your quilt top or block(s) before assembling the quilt sandwich, I strongly recommend that you quilt along the outside edges of the bias tubes, either right along the appliquéd edges (referred to as "in the ditch"), or within ⅛" of the edges. This helps to keep the design from "bubbling up" unattractively when the finished quilt is laundered.

If you have appliquéd and quilted your project in one step, you may not need to add any extra quilting at all, other than in the ditch along the seam lines of the borders.

Whichever method you have used to construct the project, you may wish to add more quilting. Echo quilting seems to be the most popular technique for highlighting appliqué, while straight-line grid work in the background and/or borders adds pleasing dimension and texture. Stippling, or other allover patterning with decorative threads, brings even more visual interest to the finished piece. Celtic knotwork and interlace designs can be used as quilting patterns as well as for appliqué. "Traditional" quilting patterns and stencils work well too, particularly in wide outer borders and in large spaces within the background.

Please don't be put off by the amount of quilting in my samples. It is not necessary to quilt everything so heavily! I happen to enjoy machine quilting—free motion quilting, particularly. So for me, in true Celtic fashion, less is not more, and more is not enough!

Space precludes a complete discussion of machine quilting techniques, but I'd like to share the procedure I use to achieve the results you see in this book. For additional information on machine quilting, I recommend Maurine Noble's *Machine Quilting Made Easy* (That Patchwork Place, 1994). See also the Bibliography on page 96.

Quilting "My Way"

I begin by looking for stabilizing lines, which I quilt in the ditch using my machine's walking foot. These lines generally run in one direction through the quilt, and are straight, or at most, very gently curved. If quilted first, these lines secure the layers by cutting down on the shifting that might occur as I scrunch and manipulate the quilt to tackle the more intricate quilting details. Border and/or sashing seams make good stabilizing lines.

Once I've quilted these key lines, I'll often echo quilt an additional line of stitches parallel to them, using either the outside or inside edge of my walking foot as a guide. The outside edge makes for a wider distance between lines of quilting, while the inside edge creates narrower chan-

nels. My preferred distance between lines of stitching is ¼" to ⅜".

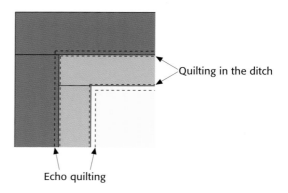

Quilting in the ditch

Echo quilting

Unless the quilt is quite large, I prefer to appliqué and quilt my bias tubes in the same step (see page 43). Once again, I use the walking foot for this. (An open-toe appliqué foot would be my second choice for this job—first choice if the sewing machine has built-in dual feed.) Although it can be a bit cumbersome, I like the way the walking foot "lifts" off the fabric with each stitch, reducing the likelihood of catching and dragging the edges of the fabric tubes.

I realize that mine is a rather unorthodox use of the walking foot, since the many sharp curves and points of Celtic-style designs require lots of turning and pivoting. For this reason, it is vital to baste all layers securely to prevent shifting and bunching, and the formation of tucks on the back of the quilt as it is steered in every direction!

> ## TIP
>
> Stop with your needle down in the fabric whenever you need to pivot around a curve or point. *Take your foot completely off the foot pedal* when adjusting the quilt. It is very easy to inadvertently nudge the foot pedal and end up stitching into the background, or worse yet, into your finger. (Don't ask me how I know this!)

If I have appliquéd the bias tubes on the top only, my next step is to quilt in the ditch with a straight stitch right along the outside edge of the appliquéd design. This is an important step, because it keeps the appliquéd areas smooth and crisp.

Regardless of whether I've quilted the appliqué before or after layering the quilt, my next step is to echo quilt ¼" to ⅜" from the outside edges of my appliquéd design, all the way around. For this quilting, I use the walking foot or, if the design is especially intricate, the darning foot. Either way, I usually echo quilt inside any large enclosed shapes as well, as shown.

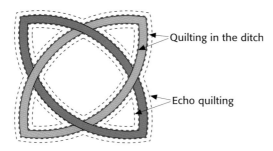

Quilting in the ditch

Echo quilting

That's the "work" part for me—now here's the "fun" part!

If there are large open spaces, I may use a stencil to transfer a quilting design. Traditional quilt stencils, such as cables or interlaced braids, are often very Celtic in appearance and work wonderfully, especially in borders. There are even a number of stencils sold specifically as "Celtic," and Hari Walner has designed continuous line stencils in various sizes that I love to use. Another great source of Celtic quilting designs is Dorothy Osler's *Quilting Design Sourcebook* (That Patchwork Place, 1996). See the bibliography and "Resources" on page 96 for additional information.

As an alternative, I might trace a part of my knotwork design on tear-away stabilizer, tissue paper, or even lightweight typing paper to stitch through for a custom quilting design. If I've been smart, I will have already considered this and will have done any necessary marking before layering my quilt sandwich. In the real world, however, I'm often making up my mind—or changing it!—as I go along.

For my *very* favorite step, I pull out my lovely rayon threads—usually variegated, but not always—and fill in all that lonely "empty" space in the quilt with free-motion quilting. If I wish to add texture, but not additional color, I use nylon monofilament thread instead.

TIP

If the piece is intended as a table runner or couch throw and likely to be laundered frequently, I tend to avoid using rayon thread. In fact, I generally limit the amount of decorative quilting I add, opting instead for more functional quilting that will still complement the appliquéd design, but will also add durability.

Depending on the style of the design, character of the fabrics, and mood of the moment, I may do one or more of the following:

Stipple: These curvy lines adds lots of texture but don't call attention to themselves. Stippling is wonderful for more formal pieces.

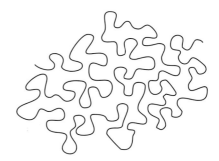

Stippling

Geometric fill: This is similar to stippling, but with straight, lightning-like lines instead of curves. I think it tends to be a little more interesting than traditional stippling by conveying a feeling of energy, excitement, and movement.

Geometric fill

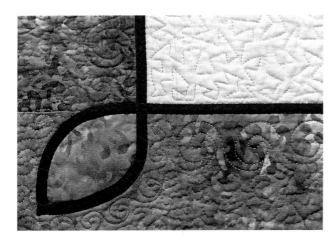

Spirals: These can be uniform in size, but tend to be more exciting when they vary to form secondary patterns in relationship to each other. Spirals were enormously significant to the ancient Celts, as well as to the pre-Celtic inhabitants of Ireland, so I also appreciate the historical aspect of using spirals.

Spirals

Crescents and spirals: These are very free form, energetic, and unpredictable. They are especially effective in larger areas, where there is room to develop rhythm.

Crescents and spirals

I may also use straight-line channel quilting or grids, particularly in the outer borders of quilts that have been heavily quilted in the center. This helps ease in any fullness or rippling that might have occurred when the center "took up," or shrank, due to the dense quilting. I use my machine's walking foot for these lines, either marking them with washable graphite, soapstone, or chalk (see page 9) or using a quilting guide that attaches to the walking foot itself.

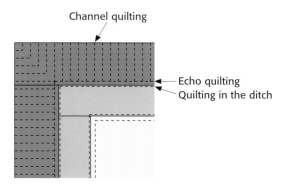

Channel quilting

Echo quilting
Quilting in the ditch

A Few Things to Remember When Quilting by Machine

Here are a few final tips to help you along.

※ Whatever quilting you choose to do, plan to distribute it evenly across the quilt. If one area is quilted very heavily and another is not, it is unlikely that your finished quilt will lie flat.

※ Be sure to bring up the bobbin thread through all layers before beginning to stitch, and to "lock," or secure, beginning and ending stitches (see "The Stitching Process" on page 22). The exception: if you are beginning at an outermost edge of the quilt sandwich, draw the top and the bobbin thread underneath the presser foot and hold them until you have taken the first few stitches. This line of stitching will be "locked" when you bind the quilt.

※ As you stitch, look ahead to where you plan to quilt next, *not* at the needle. This is trickier than it sounds. It takes some practice to build confidence in your hand-eye coordination.

※ When trimming threads at the end of a line of stitching, clip the top thread first, as close as you can to the surface of the quilt. Turn the quilt over and tug on the bobbin thread to pull the "whisker" of top thread into the batting.

Then hold the bobbin thread taut, and clip it as close to the quilt as possible. When the thread relaxes, it too will be drawn back into the batting.

※ BREATHE!

FINISHING TECHNIQUES
Squaring Up

When you are finished with the quilting, lay the quilt sandwich on a clean work surface or floor. Does it lie flat? While some fullness may be tamed by blocking the quilt after you wash it, you may wish to consider adding a bit more quilting to any "puffy" areas. Are the edges straight? Use your rotary ruler to make sure that the corners form true 90-degree angles and that the quilt's edges are indeed straight. If they are not, you'll need to "sliver trim" them into shape. Slide your cutting mat under the quilt, positioning it beneath those areas that need to be straightened. Use your rotary cutter and ruler to trim them. Don't worry about cutting across quilting lines. All lines of stitching will be secured when you attach the binding.

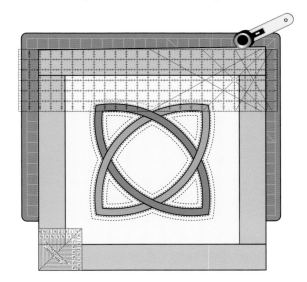

Measure the top and bottom edges of the quilt. The measurements should be equal. Do the same for the side edges. Finally, measure across the quilt diagonally from corner to corner. Once again, these measurements should agree. If they do not, trim carefully until they do.

Adding a Sleeve

I'm sure I needn't remind a quilter never to nail or staple a quilt to the wall! There are alternatives, such as special clamps that mount on the wall and hold the quilt, but some of these don't distribute the quilt's weight evenly, or may obscure the top edge of the quilt.

My preferred method for hanging a quilt is to add a fabric sleeve to the quilt back. Most quilt shows require a 3" to 4" sleeve for displaying quilts, so by adding a sleeve, my quilts are always "show ready." I also find a sleeve handy for hanging pieces at home.

1. Cut the sleeve 9" by the width of the quilt's top edge. This makes a sleeve that finishes 4" wide. If you prefer a 3"-wide sleeve, cut the sleeve 7" rather than 9".

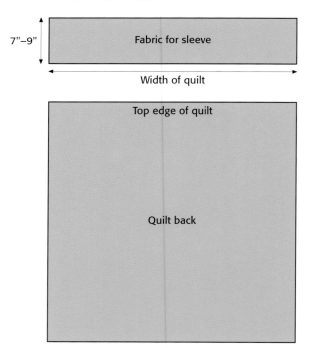

2. Turn the short raw edges to form a ⅜"-wide hem on the wrong side of the sleeve fabric and press. Repeat, turning the folded ends a second time and pressing as before. Topstitch the folds to finish the short edges.

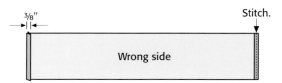

3. Fold the fabric in half, right side out, aligning the long raw edges. Press. Pin the folded sleeve in place, matching the raw edges of the sleeve with the top raw edge of the quilt back. The quilt should extend approximately ¾" beyond the sleeve at either end.

4. Machine stitch the top edge of the sleeve in place, using a scant ¼"-wide seam allowance. This seam will be covered when you add the binding.

5. Hand stitch the other edges of the sleeve to the quilt back. Make sure that your stitches do not go through to the front of the quilt—and that you do not sew the sleeve ends closed!

My favorite display method is invisible from the front, with the quilt lying flush against the wall. I have a 2½"- to 3"-wide wooden lattice or molding strip cut to the same length as the finished sleeve and add eyelet screws to either end. I thread the strip through the sleeve and hook the screws over nails I have placed in the wall. To minimize wear and tear on the wall, I use the smallest nails capable of supporting the quilt's weight.

The eyelet screws are completely hidden underneath the quilt, between the edge of the hanging sleeve and the binding.

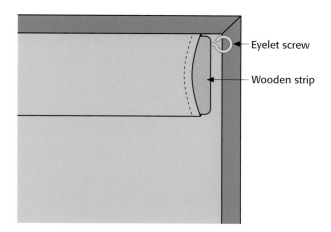

Eyelet screw

Wooden strip

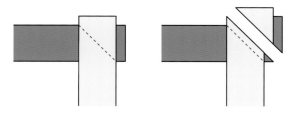

TIP

A decorative curtain rod makes a nice alternative to lattice for displaying wall hangings and other small quilt projects.

Binding

Since the edges of the quilts in this book are all straight edges, I suggest that you cut the binding fabric on the crosswise straight of grain, from selvage to selvage, rather than on the bias.

I tend to prefer a fairly narrow binding, that is, one that is comparable to the width of the interlacing bias tubes. For a double-fold binding that finishes ⅜" wide, you will need to cut all binding strips 2½" wide.

1. Cut the required number of binding strips as indicated in the specific project instructions. Join the binding strips with a diagonal seam. Press the seams open.

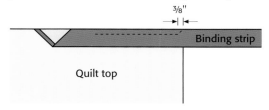

2. Fold the binding strip in half lengthwise with wrong sides together, and press.

Fold line

3. Open the binding strip at its starting end and fold the lower corner inward to create a 45-degree angle. Trim away the tip of the triangle that is formed inside the binding, leaving a ¼" seam allowance. Refold the binding strip.

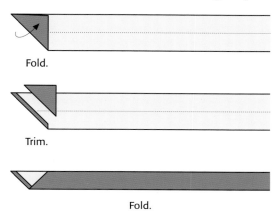

Fold.

Trim.

Fold.

4. Beginning at an inconspicuous spot along one of the quilt's side edges, test the binding by laying it around the perimeter of the quilt. Make sure that the binding seams do not fall on the corners of the quilt. When you are satisfied with the placement, turn the binding face down on the quilt top, aligning the raw edges of the binding with the raw edges of the quilt sandwich.

5. Leaving the first 5" unsewn, stitch the binding to the quilt, using a ⅜"-wide seam allowance. A walking foot will help to keep the binding from becoming stretched or distorted while you sew.

6. Stop stitching ⅜" from the first corner. With the needle down, pivot the quilt, and stitch straight off the corner at a 45-degree angle.

⅜"

Binding strip

Quilt top

7. Fold the binding strip up and away from the corner at a 45-degree angle, then fold it back down, even with the adjacent edge. This creates a pleat in the binding. Make sure that the pleat is straight, and even with the edge of the quilt.

Holding the thread out of the way, slide the corner of the quilt back under the presser foot. Beginning right at the edge of the quilt, resume sewing in the same manner around the remaining edges and corners of the quilt. Stop several inches before reaching the binding's starting point. Stop with the needle down, and keep the presser foot down as well.

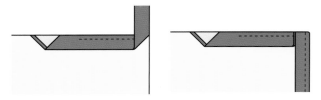

8. Open the fold at the beginning of the binding, and tuck the end of the binding inside to determine how much excess length can be trimmed. Trim the excess, making sure that the beginning and ending of the binding overlap each other approximately 1".

9. Tuck the end back inside the fold so that no cut edges are exposed. Finish sewing the binding seam.

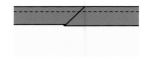

10. Turn the folded edge of the binding over the raw edge of the quilt and hand stitch in place to the back of the quilt. The binding should cover the line of machine stitching that attached the binding to the quilt top. Make sure that your stitches do not go through to the front of the quilt.

TIP

If your stitches go through all three layers as you hand stitch bindings to the back of your quilts, try switching to a finer needle. This works well, especially if you are using a tightly woven fabric, such as a batik, for the binding.

11. As you come to the corners, stitch down the binding miters on both the front and back of the quilt.

TIP

I find it easier to get a perfectly flat mitered corner on my binding if I trim a tiny triangle from the corner of the quilt sandwich. This reduces the bulk in that area and makes the corner easier to turn.

12. Hand stitch the tucked end of the binding closed.

Washing and Blocking
the Finished Quilt

The first thing I do when I complete a quilt is wash it. This removes any stiffness, as well as dust, cat hair, and other "foreign matter." It also allows the stitching to sink into the batting, creating a softer, finished look. A quilt that has been machine quilted with nylon monofilament thread, in particular, looks much better after it has been washed. Methods for washing and drying quilts can be somewhat controversial, so use the method that works best for you. If you'd like to try my method for washing my newer (non-antique) quilts, this is what you'll want to do:

1. Wash the quilt in the washing machine, in warm water, on the gentle cycle. Synthrapol or Orvus quilt soap are my favorite products for laundering my quilts.
2. Dry the quilt in the dryer on a gentle setting. Remove it while it is still slightly damp.
3. Lay the slightly damp quilt on a clean cotton blanket or mattress pad to finish drying. Make sure that the quilt is spread perfectly flat, the edges perfectly straight, the corners square, and the quilted areas free from distortion. Use a steam iron to gently coax the damp quilt into shape if necessary. Allow the blocked quilt to dry *completely* before disturbing it.

TIP

✖ Try not to fold quilts that have been heavily quilted. When possible, store them flat, layered if necessary, on an extra guest bed. You can also hang them on the wall, or roll them, right side out, on large tubes that have been covered with muslin.

✖ Periodically air and rotate your quilts, whether they are stored flat, rolled, or hung. These precautions can reduce strain on decorative stitching and prevent permanent fold lines from developing.

Signing and Labeling
Your Finished Project

Don't forget to sign and date your work! You can write directly on the front and/or the back of the quilt with permanent, nonfading, waterproof ink. You can also attach a permanent label to the back of your quilt. Consider including at least the following information: title of the quilt, name of the maker, name of the designer (if other than the maker), and when and where the quilt was made. You might also wish to note the name of the person for whom the quilt was made (if the quilt is a gift), and any additional information concerning the inspiration behind or special significance of the quilt. Posterity will thank you!

Enhancing a Traditional Quilt Pattern
with Celtic Motifs
"Irish Chain" by Nancy M. Roelfsema, 1999, Grand Rapids, Michigan, 66" x 88". Appliqué by Beth Ann Williams. Appliquéd Celtic motifs are repeated in the quilting of this well-loved traditional pattern. Collection of Nancy M. Roelfsema.

True Lover's Knot

*T*he continuous line that forms this design is symbolic of the eternal nature of true love, that is, love without end. Various versions of the True Lover's Knot can be found not only on ancient Celtic artifacts, but on articles made through the present day. It was in common use as a quilting pattern in the late nineteenth and early twentieth centuries, particularly in the English North Country, although many traditional American quilts, including many Amish quilts, also incorporate this lovely motif. The sample was finished as a small wall hanging, but it would work equally well as a decorative pillow or as a repeat block in a bed quilt. The design may be set straight or turned on-point.

Materials: 42"-wide fabric

1 fat quarter light fabric for background
1 fat quarter medium or dark print fabric for
    appliqué (bias tubes)
1 fat quarter contrasting print fabric for border
⅝ yd. fabric for backing and sleeve
¼ yd. fabric for binding
18" x 18" square of low-loft batting
Large sheet (11½" x 11½" minimum) of tracing
    paper
Fusible product

Cutting

All measurements include ¼"-wide
seam allowances.

From the light fabric, cut:
    1 square, 11½" x 11½", for background
From the contrasting print fabric, cut:
    2 strips, 3" x 11½", for side borders
    2 strips, 3" x 16½", for top and bottom borders
From the backing fabric, cut:
    1 square, 20" x 20", for backing
    1 strip, 9" x 16", for sleeve
From the binding fabric, cut:
    2 strips, each 2½" x 42", for binding

Preparing for Appliqué

Refer to "Basic Steps in Creating Celtic-Style Appliqué" on pages 11–35 for general preparation and stitching techniques. Since this is a small project, it is a good opportunity to experiment with appli-quéing and quilting in one step. The following instructions are written for that method of construction. If, however, you prefer to appliqué the design onto the quilt top only, then layer and quilt in the traditional manner, please feel free to do so (see "Appliquéing the Design" on pages 21–24 for specifics regarding differences in technique). In other words, choose the method most comfortable to you!

1. Fold and press the 11½" background square to set the guide marks for centering the appliqué pattern as described in "Preparing the Background Fabric" on page 12.

2. Fold an 11½" piece of tracing paper in the same manner as the background fabric. Align the center marking of the pattern on page 39 with the fold lines on the tracing paper. Trace the pattern onto the paper. Turn the tracing paper *top to bottom* and trace the rest of the pattern, carefully aligning the center marking and registration lines and joining the sections at the dotted lines as indicated. If you turn the tracing paper in this manner, the "unders" and "overs" of the design will flow correctly from one side of the midpoint to the other.

3. Using the guide marks to center the design, transfer the traced pattern to the 11½" background square (see "Transferring the Pattern to Fabric" on page 13).

4. Determine the total number of bias strips required for this project (see "Preparing the Bias Tubes" on page 14). Use the fat quarter of medium or dark print fabric to cut the required number of strips. Cut strips either 1" or 1¼" wide depending upon the method (and foot attachment) you will be using to construct the fabric tubes. Sew and press the fabric tubes.

5. Refer to "'Basting' the Appliqué Design" on page 18 to select the fusing method of your choice. I recommend using Steam-A-Seam2 for this project, although you may choose an alternative method if you wish.

6. Bond the bias tubes in place over the design you have marked on the background fabric.

Adding the Border

Refer to "Butted (or Squared) Borders" on page 24 for detailed instruction as needed.

1. With right sides together, pin a 3" x 11½" side border strip to the left and right sides of the appliquéd block, aligning the long raw edges. Sew the border strips to the block using a ¼"-wide seam. Press the seams toward the border strips.

2. Repeat to add the 3" x 16½" top and bottom border strips to the top and bottom edges of the block. Press.

Appliquéing and Quilting in One Step

1. Refer to "Basting the Quilt Sandwich" on page 26. Use your preferred method to layer and baste the quilt top, batting, and backing. Since this is a small project, you may wish to use a quilt basting spray rather than one of the more traditional methods.

2. Stitching through all layers of the quilt sandwich, appliqué the bias tubes. Use nylon monofilament thread and an "invisible" appliqué stitch.

3. Add additional quilting as desired. On the sample, I quilted in the ditch and echo quilted the border seams. Finally, I stipple quilted the background. (It didn't really need the stippling. I just had fun doing it!) Refer to "Choosing a Quilting Method" on page 27 for additional guidance as needed.

Watercolor/Impressionistic Techniques Enhanced with Celtic Motifs

"Faerie Wood" by Beth Ann Williams, Grand Rapids, Michigan, 1999, 30" x 39". This impressionistic scene evokes visions of faeries dancing in a hidden forest glade.

Finishing

1. Trim the batting and backing even with the edges of the quilt top. Square up the quilt as necessary.

2. Use the 9" x 16" strip of backing fabric to construct and sew a hanging sleeve to the back of the quilt sandwich.

3. Use the 2½" x 42" strips to make binding. Bind the quilt to finish.

4. Sign or make a label for your finished quilt.

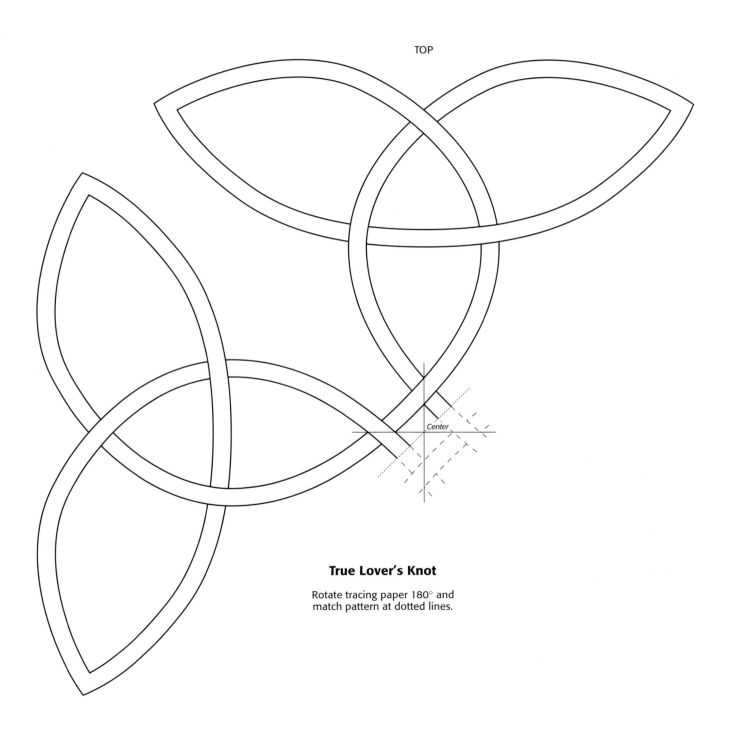

TOP

Center

True Lover's Knot

Rotate tracing paper 180° and
match pattern at dotted lines.

Thinking of Danyelle

This is the first of three little quilts I've made from the same Celtic-style design (see "Afro-Celt" on page 44 and "Stained Glass Window" on page 48). This version is owned by Danyelle Glazier.

Materials: 42"-wide fabric

⅝ yd. light fabric for background
⅛ yd. *each* of 3 fabrics for appliqué insets
1 fat quarter fabric *each* of 2 contrasting fabrics
  for appliqué (bias tubes)
¼ yd. medium solid or subtle print fabric for
  inner border*
¼ yd. multicolored print for appliqué accent
  border
¼ yd. dark solid or subtle print for outer border
⅞ yd. fabric for backing and sleeve
¼ yd. fabric for binding
24" x 26" piece of low-loft batting
Large sheet (17" x 18½" minimum) of tracing
  paper
Fusible product
*May be either traditional (9" x 42") or fat (18"
  x 22") quarter yard.

Cutting

*All measurements include ¼"-wide
seam allowances.*

From the light fabric, cut:
  1 piece, 17" x 18½", for background
From the medium fabric, cut:
  2 strips, each 1½" x 18½", for side inner
    borders
  2 strips, each 1½" x 19, for top and bottom
    inner borders
From the multicolored print, cut:
  2 strips, each 1¼" x 23½", for side accent
    borders
  2 strips, each 1¼" x 22", for top and bottom
    accent borders
From the dark fabric, cut:
  2 strips, each 2" x 20½", for side outer borders
  2 strips, each 2" x 22", for top and bottom outer
    borders
From the backing fabric, cut
  1 piece, 26" x 28", for backing
  1 strip, 9" x 22", for sleeve
From the binding fabric, cut:
  3 strips, each 2½" x 42", for binding

Preparing for Appliqué

Refer to "Basic Steps in Creating Celtic-Style Appliqué" on pages 11–35 for general preparation and stitching techniques. Since this is a fairly small project, it is a good opportunity to experiment with appliquéing and quilting in one step. The following instructions are written for that method of construction. If, however, you prefer to appliqué the design onto the quilt top only, then layer and quilt in the traditional manner, please feel free to do so (see "Appliquéing the Design" on pages 21–24 for specifics regarding differences in technique). In other words, choose the method most comfortable to you!

1. Fold and press the 17" x 18½" background piece to set the guide marks for centering the appliqué pattern as described in "Preparing the Background Fabric" on page 12.

2. Fold a 17" x 18½" piece of tracing paper in the same manner as the background fabric. Align the center marking of the pattern on page 51 with the fold lines on the tracing paper. Trace the pattern onto the paper. Turn the tracing paper as directed and trace the rest of the pattern, carefully aligning the center marking and registration lines and joining the sections at the dotted lines as indicated. If you turn the tracing paper in this manner, the "unders" and "overs" of the design will flow correctly.

3. Using the guide marks to center the design, transfer the traced pattern to the 17" x 18½" background piece (see "Transferring the Pattern to Fabric" on page 13).

4. Refer to "Placing the Fabric Insets" on page 13. Refer to the placement diagram on page 12 and use your pattern to prepare the insets for bonding. Trace inset pieces A–E onto your preferred fusible. Don't forget to add seam allowances.

From inset fabric #1, cut 6 each of A and B and 1 of E. From inset fabric #2, cut 6 of C. From inset fabric #3, cut 6 of D.

5. Beginning with the outermost insets (A and B), bond the insets to the design you have marked on the background fabric, using the placement diagram below and the quilt photo for guidance.

Placement Diagram

6. Referring to the placement diagram and the quilt photo, determine the total number of bias strips *of each color* required for this project (see "Preparing the Bias Tubes" on page 14). Use the two fat quarters of contrasting fabrics to cut the required number of strips. Cut strips either 1" or 1¼" wide depending upon the method (and foot attachment) you will be using to construct the fabric tubes. Sew and press the fabric tubes.

7. Refer to "'Basting' the Appliqué Design" on page 18 to select the fusing method of your choice. I recommend using Steam-A-Seam2 for this project, although you may choose an alternative method if you wish.

8. Bond the bias tubes in place over the design you have marked on the background fabric.

Adding the Inner and Outer Borders

Refer to "Butted (or Squared) Borders" on page 24 for detailed instruction as needed.

1. With right sides together, pin a 1½" x 18½" side inner border strip to the left and right sides of the appliquéd block, aligning the long raw edges. Sew the border strips to the block, using a ¼"-wide seam allowance. Press the seams toward the border strips.

2. Repeat to add the 1½" x 19" top and bottom inner border strips to the top and bottom edges of the block. Press.

3. In the same fashion, add the 2" x 20½" side and 2" x 22" top and bottom outer border strips to the appropriate sides of the quilt. Press the seams toward the outer border.

Adding the Appliqué Accent Border

You will be using fabric strips that you have cut on the crosswise straight of grain to construct the tubes for the appliqué accent border. Since these accent lines must be straight, bias tubes are not desirable.

1. Fold the 1¼"-wide accent border strips in half, wrong sides together, aligning the long raw edges.

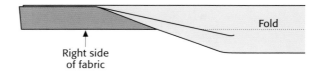

Fold

Right side of fabric

2. Stitch down the long raw edge, taking a scant ¼" seam allowance.

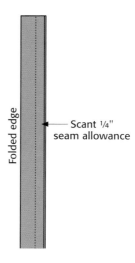

Folded edge

Scant ¼" seam allowance

3. Use bias press bars to press the tubes flat, just as you would for bias tubes. You do not need to center or trim the seam allowance, as long as it is not visible when the tubes are pressed.

4. Use Steam-A-Seam2 or your preferred fusible to bond the 23½"-long tubes to the side borders and the 22"-long tubes to the top and bottom borders of the quilt. Use the outside seam of the inner border as a guide for placing the outer edge of each tube. The tube will cover approximately ⅜" of the inner border.

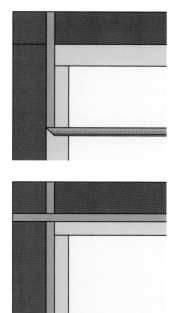

5. Appliqué the tubes to the quilt.

> **TIP**
>
> If you prefer, you may appliqué the accent border strips after the quilt sandwich has been assembled. See "Appliquéing and Quilting in One Step" (at right).

Appliquéing and Quilting in One Step

1. Refer to "Basting the Quilt Sandwich" on page 26. Use your preferred method to layer and baste the quilt top, batting, and backing. Since this is a fairly small project, you may wish to use a quilt basting spray rather than one of the more traditional methods.

2. Stitching through all layers of the quilt sandwich, appliqué the bias tubes, and—if you haven't already—the accent border tubes. Use nylon monofilament thread and an "invisible" applique stitch.

3. Add additional quilting as desired. On the sample, in addition to the quilting I did in the appliqué process, I echo quilted around the appliqué design, added ditch and echo quilting in the borders and appliqué background, and traced a decorative stencil in the corners of the background block. Refer to "Choosing a Quilting Method" on page 27 for additional guidance as needed.

Finishing

1. Trim the batting and backing even with the edges of the quilt top. Square up the quilt as necessary.

2. Use the 9" x 22" strip of backing fabric to construct and sew a hanging sleeve to the back of the quilt sandwich.

3. Use the 2½" x 42" strips to make binding. Bind the quilt to finish.

4. Sign or make a label for your finished quilt.

Afro-Celt

T his is the second of three quilts I've made from the same Celtic-style design (see "Thinking of Danyelle" on page 40 and "Stained Glass Window" on page 48). Although I've used it here as the centerpiece for a wall hanging, this version of the design would also make a great decorative pillow or repeat block for a bed quilt.

Materials: 42"-wide fabric

⅝ yd. dark solid, hand-dye, or subtle print for
  background
1 fat quarter *each* of 3 bright fabrics for appliqué
  (bias tubes)
¼ yd. medium print for inner border*
¼ yd. bright contrasting solid or subtle print for
  accent "flap" border
⅝ yd. bright African print for outer border
1 yd. fabric for backing and sleeve
¼ yd. fabric for binding
30" x 32" piece of low-loft batting
Large sheet (17½" x 19" minimum) of tracing
  paper
Fusible product
*May be either traditional (9" x 42") or fat
  (18" x 22") quarter yard.

Cutting

*All measurements include ¼"-wide
seam allowances.*

From the dark solid, hand-dye, or subtle print,
  cut:
  1 piece, 17½ x 19", for background
From the medium print, cut:
  2 strips, each 1¾" x 19", for side inner borders
  2 strips, each 1¾" x 20", for top and bottom
    inner borders
From the bright contrasting solid or subtle print,
  cut:
  2 strips, each 1¼" x 21½", for side accent "flap"
    borders
  2 strips, each 1¼" x 20", for top and bottom
    accent "flap" borders
From the bright African print, cut:
  2 strips, each 4¼" x 21½", for side outer bor-
    ders
  2 strips, each 4¼" x 27½", for top and bottom
    outer borders
From the backing fabric, cut:
  1 piece, 32" x 34", for backing
  1 strip, 9" x 27½", for sleeve
From the binding fabric, cut:
  3 strips, each 2½" x 42", for binding

Preparing for Appliqué

Refer to "Basic Steps in Creating Celtic-Style
Appliqué" on pages 11–35 for general preparation and stitching techniques. Since this is a
moderately small project, it is a good opportunity to experiment with appliquéing and quilting in
one step. The following instructions are written
for that method of construction. If, however, you
prefer to appliqué the design onto the quilt top
only, then layer and quilt in the traditional manner, please feel free to do so (see "Appliquéing
the Design" on pages 21–24 for specifics regarding differences in technique). In other words,
choose the method most comfortable to you!

1. Fold and press the 17½" x 19" background
   piece to set the guide marks for centering the
   appliqué pattern as described in "Preparing
   the Background Fabric" on page 12.
2. Fold a 17½" x 19" piece of tracing paper in the
   same manner as the background fabric. Align
   the center marking of the pattern on page 51
   with the fold lines on the tracing paper. Trace
   the pattern onto the paper. Turn the tracing
   paper as directed and trace the rest of the pattern, carefully aligning the center marking
   and registration lines and joining the sections
   at the dotted lines as indicated. If you turn the
   tracing paper in this manner, the "unders" and
   "overs" of the design will flow correctly.
3. Using the guide marks to center the design,
   transfer the traced pattern to the 17½" x 19"
   background piece (see "Transferring the
   Pattern to Fabric" on page 13).
4. Referring to the placement diagram on page
   46 and the color photo on page 44, determine
   the total number of bias strips of *each color*
   required for this project (see "Preparing the
   Bias Tubes" on page 14). Use the three fat
   quarters of bright fabrics to cut the required
   number of strips. Cut strips either 1" or 1¼"
   wide depending upon the method (and foot
   attachment) you will be using to construct the
   fabric tubes. Sew and press the fabric tubes.

Placement Diagram

5. Refer to "'Basting' the Appliqué Design" on page 18 to select the fusing method of your choice. I recommend using Steam-A-Seam2 for this project, although you may choose an alternative method if you wish.

6. Bond the bias tubes in place over the design you have marked on the background fabric. Use the placement diagram and the color photo for guidance in placing the colors.

Adding the Borders

1. Refer to "Butted (or Squared) Borders" on page 24. With right sides together, pin a 1¾" x 19" side inner border strip to the left and right sides of the appliquéd block, aligning the long raw edges. Sew the border strips to the block, using a ¼"-wide seam allowance. Press the seams toward the border strips.

2. Repeat to add the 1¾" x 20" top and bottom inner border strips to the top and bottom edges of the block. Press.

3. Refer to "Narrow Accent or 'Flap' Borders" on page 25. Fold and sew the 1¼" x 21½" side accent border strips to the sides of the quilt to create "flap" borders. Repeat to fold and sew the 1¼" x 20" top and bottom accent border strips to the top and bottom edges of the quilt.

4. Sew the 4¼" x 21½" side outer borders and the 4¼" x 27½" top and bottom outer borders to the quilt as directed in "Narrow Accent or 'Flap' Borders," step 6, on page 25. Press as directed.

> **TIP**
>
> In this particular quilt, I have appliquéd the "flap" border down so that it becomes a narrow accent border.

Appliquéing and Quilting in One Step

1. Refer to "Basting the Quilt Sandwich" on page 26. Use your preferred method to layer and baste the quilt top, batting, and backing. Since this is a moderately small project, you may wish to use a quilt basting spray rather than one of the more traditional methods.

2. Stitching through all layers of the quilt sandwich, appliqué the bias tubes. Use nylon monofilament thread and an "invisible" appliqué stitch.

3. Add additional quilting as desired. On the sample, in addition to the quilting I did in the appliqué process, I quilted in the ditch and echo quilted in the borders, added geometric fill in the appliqué background, and quilted spirals and crescents in the wide outer border. Refer to "Choosing a Quilting Method" on page 27 for additional guidance as needed.

Finishing

1. Trim the batting and backing even with the edges of the quilt top. Square up the quilt as necessary.

2. Use the 9" x 27½" strip of backing fabric to construct and sew a hanging sleeve to the back of the quilt sandwich.

3. Use the 2½" x 42" strips to make binding. Bind the quilt to finish.

4. Sign or make a label for your finished quilt.

Embellishing with Free-Motion Embroidery

"Echo of the Celts" by Beth Ann Williams, Grand Rapids, Michigan, 1996, 42" x 42". I adapted the central motif—a version of the traditional "True Lover's Knot"—from the cover of a contemporary wedding photo album designed by Gail Lawther for her book, The Complete Quilting Course. The motifs around the edges of the piece are worked in gold metallic and foil thread. They are taken from my personal sketchbook of patterns and date from the early and middle stages of the La Tène style of Celtic art (about 500 B.C.–A.D. 100).

Stained Glass Window

Finished Size: 25" x 26"

*T*his wall hanging is the third of the three quilts I've made from the same Celtic-style design (see "Thinking of Danyelle" on page 40 and "Afro-Celt" on page 44).

Materials: 42"-wide fabric

⅝ yd. light fabric for background

⅛ yd. *each* of 7 jewel-tone fabrics for appliqué insets

⅝ yd. multicolored print for outer border

⅞ yd. fabric for backing and sleeve

¼ yd. fabric for binding

27" x 28" piece of low-loft batting

Large sheet (17½" x 18½" minimum) of tracing paper

One 11-yd. roll black, 100% cotton Quick-Bias fusible, ¼" wide (see page 9)

Cutting

*All measurements include ¼"-wide
seam allowances.*

From the light fabric, cut:

    1 piece, 17½" x 18½" , for background

From the multicolored print, cut:

    2 strips, each 4¼" x 18½", for side outer borders

    2 strips, each 4¼" x 25", for top and bottom outer borders

From the backing fabric, cut:

    1 piece, 29" x 30", for backing

    1 strip, 9" x 25", for sleeve

From the binding fabric, cut:

    3 strips, each 2½" x 42", for binding

Preparing for Appliqué

Refer to "Basic Steps in Creating Celtic-Style Appliqué" on pages 11–35 for general preparation and stitching techniques. Since this is a moderately small project, it is a good opportunity to experiment with appliquéing and quilting in one step. The following instructions are written for that method of construction. If, however, you prefer to appliqué the design onto the quilt top only, then layer and quilt in the traditional manner, please feel free to do so (see "Appliquéing the Design" on pages 21–24 for specifics regarding differences in technique). In other words, choose the method most comfortable to you!

1. Fold and press the 17½" x 18½" piece of background fabric to set the guide marks for centering the appliqué pattern as described in "Preparing the Background Fabric" on page 12.

2. Fold a 17½" x 18½" piece of tracing paper in the same manner as the background fabric. Align the center marking of the pattern on page 51 with the fold lines on the tracing paper. Trace the pattern onto the paper. Turn the tracing paper as directed and trace the rest of the pattern, carefully aligning the center marking and registration lines and joining the sections at the dotted lines as indicated. If you turn the tracing paper in this manner, the "unders" and "overs" of the design will flow correctly.

3. Using the guide marks to center the design, transfer the traced pattern to the 17½" x 18½" background piece (see "Transferring the Pattern to Fabric" on page 13).

4. Refer to "Placing the Fabric Insets" on page 13. Refer to the placement diagram on page 50 and use your pattern to prepare the insets for bonding. Trace inset pieces A, A reverse, B, C, D, D reverse, E, F, G, and H onto your preferred fusible. Don't forget to add seam allowances.

    From inset fabric #1, cut 6 each of A and A reverse. From inset fabric #2, cut 6 of B. From inset fabric #3, cut 6 of C. From inset fabric #4, cut 6 each of D and D reverse. From inset fabric #5, cut 6 of E. From inset fabric #6, cut 6 of F. From inset fabric #7, cut 6 of G and 1 of H.

5. Beginning with the outermost insets (A and A reverse), bond the insets to the design you have marked on the background fabric, using the placement diagram below and the color photo on page 48 for guidance.

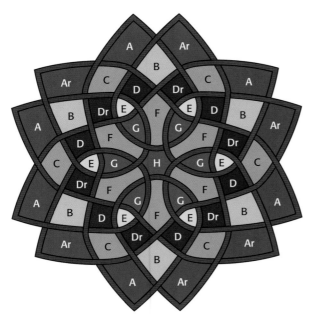

Placement Diagram

6. Referring to "Alternative 'Basting' Methods" on page 20, bond the ¼"-wide black fusible in place over the design you have marked on the background fabric.

Adding the Border

Refer to "Butted (or Squared) Borders" on page 24 for detailed instruction as needed.

1. With right sides together, pin a 4¼" x 18½" side border strip to both the left and right sides of the appliquéd block, aligning the long raw edges. Sew the border strips to the block, using a ¼"-wide seam allowance. Press the seams toward the border strips.
2. Repeat to add the 4¼" x 25" top and bottom border strips to the top and bottom edges of the block. Press.

Adding the Black Accent Strip

1. Transfer the corner pattern on page 51 to the outside edge of each corner of the background block as shown in the color photo on page 48. (You will be marking on the border.)

> **TIP**
>
> **You do not need to mark the straight sections of the appliqué accent strip, since the strip is laid right on top of the seam line (see step 2, below).**

2. Referring to "Alternative 'Basting' Methods" on page 20, bond the ¼"-wide black fusible in place over the seam line between the border and the background block, following the oval corner design you marked in step 1.

Appliquéing and Quilting in One Step

1. Refer to "Basting the Quilt Sandwich" on page 26. Use your preferred method to layer and baste the quilt top, batting, and backing. Since this is a moderately small project, you may wish to use a quilt basting spray rather than one of the more traditional methods.
2. Stitching through all layers of the quilt sandwich, appliqué the Quick-Bias to the background block and also to the border. Use smoke-colored nylon monofilament thread or 60-weight black mercerized embroidery thread and an "invisible" appliqué stitch.
3. Add additional quilting as desired. On the sample, in addition to the quilting I did in the appliqué process, I added geometric fill in the appliqué background, quilted a row of spirals next to the black accent strip on the outer border, and filled the balance of the border with stippling. Refer to "Choosing a Quilting Method" on page 27 for additional guidance as needed.

Finishing

1. Trim the batting and backing even with the edges of the quilt top. Square up the quilt as necessary.
2. Use the 9" x 25" strip of backing fabric to construct and sew a hanging sleeve to the back of the quilt sandwich.
3. Use the 2½" x 42" strips to make binding. Bind the quilt to finish.
4. Sign or make a label for your finished quilt.

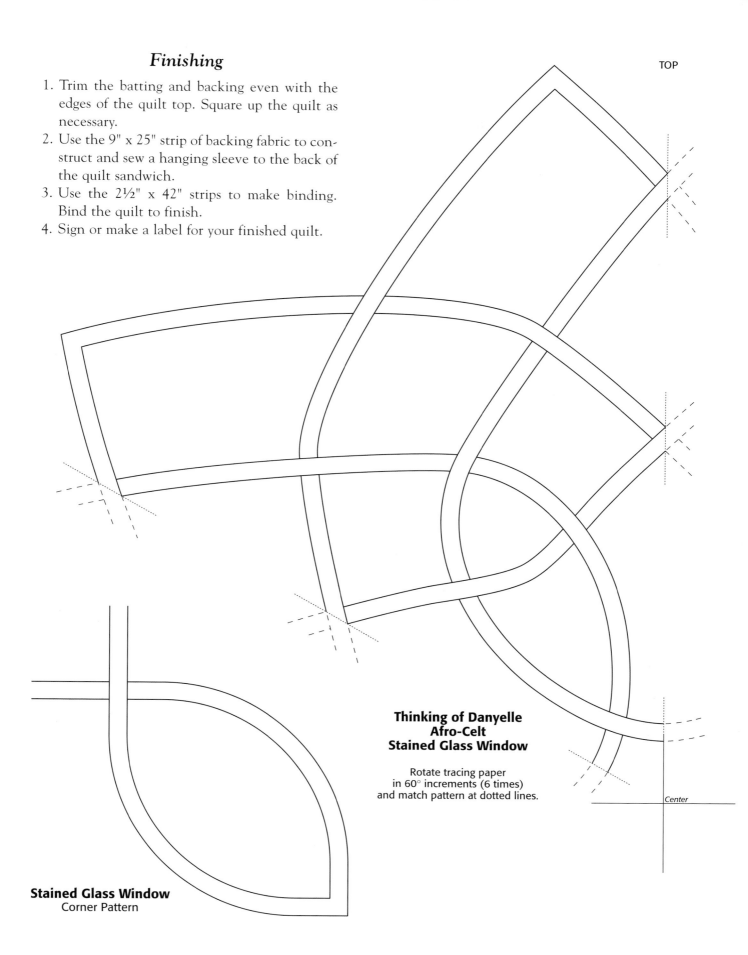

TOP

Thinking of Danyelle
Afro-Celt
Stained Glass Window

Rotate tracing paper
in 60° increments (6 times)
and match pattern at dotted lines.

Center

Stained Glass Window
Corner Pattern

Stained Glass Pillow

Finished Size: 19" x 19"

T his design highlights a large decorative pillow, perfect to tuck behind you when reading in bed. Rich batik fabrics add to the illusion of stained glass. To demonstrate the versatility of the design, I gave two versions of the line-drawn pattern to Sharon Bickel. One of the resulting wall hangings—"Anemone"—is shown on page 59.

Materials: 42"-wide fabric

1 fat quarter light fabric for background

⅛ yd. *each* of 5 brightly colored fabrics for appliqué insets

⅛ yd. medium subtle print for accent "flap" border

¼ yd. multicolored print for outer border

⅝ yd. fabric for lining

⅝ yd. fabric for backing

20" x 20" square of batting

Large piece (16" x 16" minimum) of tracing paper

Fusible product

20" pillow form

One 11-yd. roll black, 100% cotton Quick-Bias fusible, ¼" wide (see page 9)

Cutting

All measurements include ¼"-wide seam allowances.

From the light fabric, cut:

1 square, 16" x 16", for appliqué background

From the medium subtle print, cut:

4 strips, each 1¼" x 16", for accent "flap" border

From the multicolored print, cut:

2 strips, each 2¼" x 16", for side outer borders

2 strips, each 2¼" x 19½", for top and bottom outer borders

From the lining fabric, cut:

1 square, 20" x 20", for lining

From the backing fabric, cut:

2 pieces, each 19½" x 15", for pillow back

Preparing for Appliqué

Refer to "Basic Steps in Creating Celtic-Style Appliqué" on pages 11–35 for general preparation and stitching techniques. Since this is a fairly small project, it is a good opportunity to experiment with appliquéing and quilting in one step. The following instructions are written for that method of construction. If, however, you prefer to appliqué the design onto the pillow top only, then layer and quilt in the traditional manner, please feel free to do so (see "Appliquéing the Design" on pages 21–24 for specifics regarding differences in technique). In other words, choose the method most comfortable to you!

1. Fold and press the 16" square of background fabric to set the guide marks for centering the appliqué pattern as described in "Preparing the Background Fabric" on page 12.

2. Fold a 16" x 16" piece of tracing paper in the same manner as the background fabric. Align the center marking of the pattern on page 56 with the fold lines on the tracing paper. Trace the pattern onto the paper. Turn the tracing paper as directed and trace the rest of the pattern, carefully aligning the center marking and registration lines and joining the sections at the dotted lines as indicated. If you turn the tracing paper in this manner, the "unders" and "overs" of the design will flow correctly.

3. Using the guide marks to center the design, transfer the traced pattern to the 16" square of background fabric (see "Transferring the Pattern to Fabric" on page 13).

4. Refer to "Placing the Fabric Insets" on page 13. Refer to the placement diagram below and use your pattern to prepare the insets for bonding. Trace inset pieces A, B, B reverse, C, D, and E onto your preferred fusible. Don't forget to add seam allowances.

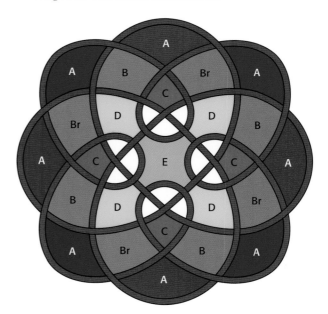

Placement Diagram

From inset fabric #1, cut 4 of A. From inset fabric #2, cut 4 of A. From inset fabric #3, cut 4 of B and 4 of B reverse. From inset fabric #4, cut 4 of C. From inset fabric #5, cut 4 of D and 1 of E.

5. Beginning with the outermost insets (A), bond the insets to the design you have marked on the background fabric, using the placement diagram on page 53 and the color photo on page 52 for guidance.

6. Referring to "Alternative 'Basting' Methods" on page 20, bond the ¼"-wide black fusible in place over the design you have marked on the background fabric.

Adding the Borders

1. Refer to "Narrow Accent or 'Flap' Borders" on page 25. Fold and sew a 1¼" x 16" side accent border strip to the left and right sides of the block to create "flap" borders. Repeat to fold and sew the remaining 1¼" x 16" top accent border strips to the top and bottom edges of the block.

2. Sew the 2¼" x 16" side outer borders and the 2¼" x 19½" top and bottom outer borders to the quilt as directed in "Narrow Accent or 'Flap' Borders," step 6, on page 25. Press as directed.

TIP

In this project, I left the flap free, for a three-dimensional accent.

Appliquéing and Quilting in One Step

1. Refer to "Basting the Quilt Sandwich" on page 26. Use your preferred method to layer and baste the pillow top, batting, and lining. Since this is a fairly small project, you may wish to use a quilt basting spray rather than one of the more traditional methods.

2. Stitching through all layers of the quilt sandwich, appliqué the Quick-Bias to the background block. Use smoke-colored nylon monofilament thread or 60-weight black mercerized embroidery thread and an "invisible" appliqué stitch.

3. Add additional quilting as desired. On the sample, in addition to the quilting I did in the appliqué process, I echo quilted around the appliqué design and added ditch and echo quilting in the borders and appliqué background. Refer to "Choosing a Quilting Method" on page 27 for additional guidance as needed.

Making the Block into a Pillow

1. Trim the batting and lining fabric even with the pillow top. Square up the pillow top as necessary.

2. Turn one long raw edge over twice to form a ⅜"-wide hem on the wrong side of each 19½" x 15" backing piece, and press. Topstitch the folds to finish them.

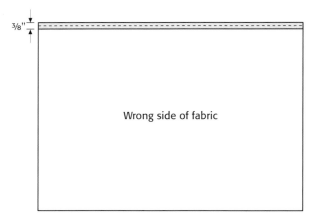

⅜"

Wrong side of fabric

3. Place the quilted pillow top and one hemmed backing panel right sides together, aligning the long unfinished edge of the backing panel with the *top* raw edge of the pillow top.

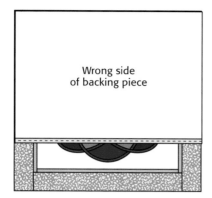

Wrong side of backing piece

4. Place the remaining hemmed backing panel right sides together with the quilted pillow top, this time aligning the long unfinished edge of the backing panel with the *bottom* raw edge of the pillow top. The hemmed edges of the two backing panels will overlap.

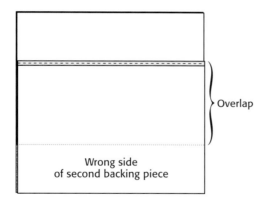

Overlap

Wrong side of second backing piece

5. Pin generously. Transfer the pattern on page 56 to your preferred template material to make a curved corner template. Use the template to mark a curve at each corner of the pillow backing. Trim away the excess fabric, making sure to cut through all three layers.

6. Stitch completely around the outside edge of the pillow using a ⅜"-wide seam allowance. Reinforce the hemmed edges of the pillow back by stitching over those areas three times.

Reinforce.   Reinforce.

7. Use a zigzag stitch (or your serger) to finish the raw edges of the seam around the entire pillow. This prevents the seam from raveling when the pillow cover is washed.

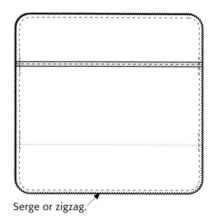

Serge or zigzag.

8. Turn the pillow cover right side out. Insert the pillow form, carefully smoothing the pillow covering to eliminate lumping or bunching of the batting and lining.

TIP

I prefer to use a pillow form that is slightly larger than the pillow cover to make a nice, plump pillow!

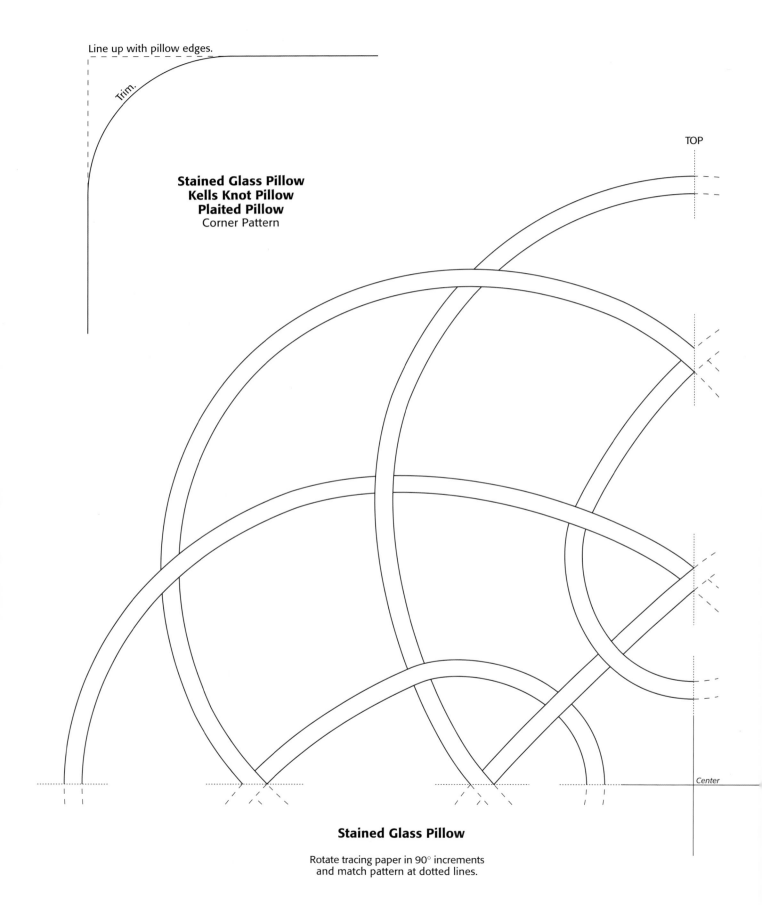

Line up with pillow edges.

Trim.

**Stained Glass Pillow
Kells Knot Pillow
Plaited Pillow**
Corner Pattern

TOP

Center

Stained Glass Pillow

Rotate tracing paper in 90° increments
and match pattern at dotted lines.

Kells Knot Pillow

Finished Size: 13 ¼" x 13 ¼"

*T*his pillow sports a classic Celtic knot found in the Book of Kells. This design would also make a lovely little wall hanging or repeat block for a bed quilt.

Materials: 42"-wide fabric

1 fat quarter light fabric for background
1 fat quarter contrasting fabric for appliqué (bias
    tubes)
1 fat quarter fabric for lining
⅓ yd. fabric for backing
15" x 15" square of batting
Large sheet (14" x 14" minimum) of tracing
    paper
Fusible product
14" pillow form

Cutting

*All measurements include ¼"-wide
seam allowances.*

From the light fabric, cut:
    1 square, 14" x 14", for background
From the lining fabric, cut:
    1 square, 15" x 15", for lining
From the backing fabric, cut:
    2 rectangles, each 14" x 10", for pillow back

Preparing for Appliqué

Refer to "Basic Steps in Creating Celtic-Style Appliqué" on pages 11–35 for general preparation and stitching techniques. Since this is a small project, it is a good opportunity to experiment with appliquéing and quilting in one step. The following instructions are written for that method of construction. If, however, you prefer to appliqué the design onto the pillow top only, then layer and quilt in the traditional manner, please feel free to do so (see "Appliquéing the Design" on pages 21–24 for specifics regarding differences in technique). In other words, choose the method most comfortable to you!

1. Fold and press the 14" background square to set the guide marks for centering the appliqué pattern as described in "Preparing the Background Fabric" on page 12.

2. Fold a 14" square of tracing paper in the same manner as the background fabric. Align the center marking of the pattern on page 60 with the fold lines on the tracing paper. Trace the pattern onto the paper. Turn the tracing paper

top to bottom and repeat to trace the other half of the pattern, carefully aligning the center marking and registration lines, and joining the sections at the dotted lines as indicated. If you turn the tracing paper in this manner, the "unders" and "overs" of the design will flow correctly from one side of the midpoint to the other.

3. Using the guide marks to center the design, transfer the traced pattern to the 14" square of background fabric (see "Transferring the Pattern to Fabric" on page 13).

4. Determine the total number of bias strips required for this project (see "Preparing the Bias Tubes" on page 14). Use the fat quarter of contrasting fabric to cut the required number of strips. Strips will be cut either 1" or 1¼" wide depending upon the method (and foot attachment) you will be using to construct the fabric tubes. Sew and press the fabric tubes.

5. Refer to "'Basting' the Appliqué Design" on page 18 to select the fusing method of your choice. I recommend using Steam-A-Seam2 for this project, although you may choose an alternative method if you wish.

6. Bond the bias tubes in place over the design you have marked on the background fabric.

Appliquéing and Quilting in One Step

1. Refer to "Basting the Quilt Sandwich" on page 26. Use your preferred method to layer and baste the pillow top, batting, and lining. Since this is a small project, you may wish to use a quilt basting spray rather than one of the more traditional methods.

2. Stitching through all layers of the quilt sandwich, appliqué the bias tubes. Use nylon monofilament thread and an "invisible" appliqué stitch.

3. Add additional quilting as desired. On the sample, in addition to the quilting I did in the appliqué process, I echo quilted around the appliqué design. Refer to "Choosing a Quilting Method" on page 27 for additional guidance as needed.

Making the Block into a Pillow

Refer to "Making the Block into a Pillow" on pages 54–55. Follow steps 1 through 8 to assemble a pillow using the quilted Kells Knot block, the two 14" x 10" backing pieces, and the 14" pillow form.

Placement Diagram

"Anemone," by Sharon L. Bickel, 1999, Wyoming, Michigan, 25¼" x 25¼". Appliqué design by Beth Ann Williams. This wall hanging was made from the same pattern as "Stained Glass Pillow" on page 52, this time with points instead of loops on the outer edge. Collection of Sharon L. Bickel.

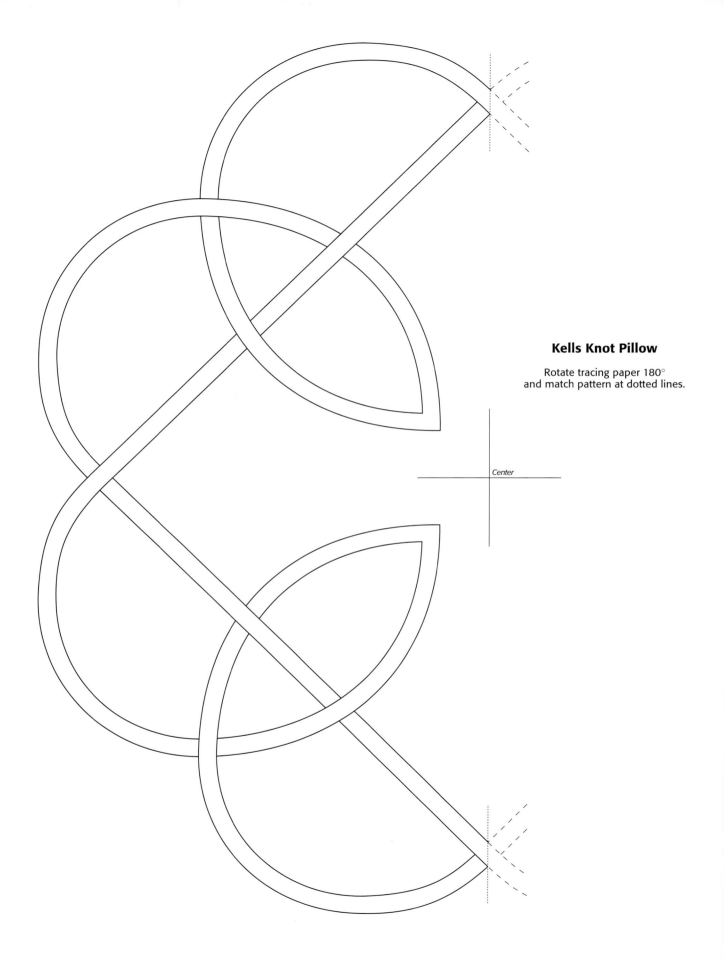

Kells Knot Pillow

Rotate tracing paper 180°
and match pattern at dotted lines.

Center

Plaited Pillow

Celtic knotwork is based on plaits, this example more clearly than most. Like "Kells Knot" on page 57, this motif is used here to decorate a pillow, but it would also make an attractive small wall hanging or repeat block for a bed quilt.

Materials: 42"-wide fabric

1 fat quarter light fabric for background
6" x 6" square contrasting fabric for appliqué
    insets
1 fat quarter *each* of 2 subtle print fabrics for
    appliqué (bias tubes)
1 fat quarter fabric for lining
⅓ yd. fabric for backing
15" x 15" square of batting
Large sheet (14" x 14" minimum) of tracing
    paper
Fusible product
14" pillow form

Cutting

*All measurements include ¼"-wide
seam allowances.*

From the light fabric, cut:
    1 square, 14" x 14", for background
From the lining fabric, cut:
    1 square, 15" x 15", for lining
From the backing fabric, cut:
    2 pieces, each 14" x 10", for pillow back

Preparing for Appliqué

Refer to "Basic Steps in Creating Celtic-Style Appliqué" on pages 11–35 for general preparation and stitching techniques. Since this is a small project, it is a good opportunity to experiment with appli-quéing and quilting in one step. The following instructions are written for that method of construction. If, however, you prefer to appliqué the design onto the pillow top only, then layer and quilt in the traditional manner, please feel free to do so (see "Appliquéing the Design" on pages 21–24 for specifics regarding differences in technique). In other words, choose the method most comfortable to you!

1. Fold and press the 14" background square to set the guide marks for centering the appliqué pattern as described in "Preparing the Background Fabric" on page 12.

2. Fold a 14" square of tracing paper in the same manner as the background fabric. Align the center marking of the pattern on page 64 with the fold lines on the tracing paper. Trace the pattern onto the paper. Turn the tracing paper *top to bottom* and repeat to trace the other half of the pattern, carefully aligning the center marking and registration lines and joining the sections at the dotted lines as indicated. If you turn the tracing paper in this manner, the "unders" and "overs" of the design will flow correctly from one side of the midpoint to the other.

3. Using the guide marks to center the design, transfer the traced pattern to the 14" square of background fabric (see "Transferring the Pattern to Fabric" on page 13).

4. Refer to "Placing the Fabric Insets" on page 13. Refer to the placement diagram below and use your pattern to prepare the insets for bonding. Trace inset piece A onto your preferred fusible. Don't forget to add seam allowances. From the inset fabric, cut 5 of A.

5. Bond the insets to the design you have marked on the background fabric, using the placement diagram below and the color photo on page 61 for guidance.

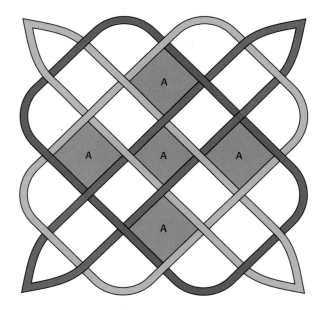

Placement Diagram

6. Referring to the placement diagram, determine the total number of bias strips of *each color* required for this project (see "Preparing the Bias Tubes" on page 14). Use the fat quarters of subtle print fabrics to cut the required number of strips. Strips will be cut either 1" or 1¼" wide depending upon the method (and foot attachment) you will be using to construct the fabric tubes. Sew and press the fabric tubes.

7. Refer to "'Basting' the Appliqué Design" on page 18 to select the fusing method of your choice. I recommend using Steam-A-Seam2 for this project, although you may choose an alternative method if you wish.

8. Bond the bias tubes in place over the design you have marked on the background fabric.

Appliquéing and Quilting in One Step

1. Refer to "Basting the Quilt Sandwich" on page 26. Use your preferred method to layer and baste the pillow top, batting, and lining. Since this is a small project, you may wish to use a quilt basting spray rather than one of the more traditional methods.

2. Stitching through all layers of the quilt sandwich, appliqué the bias tubes. Use nylon monofilament thread and an "invisible" appliqué stitch.

3. Add additional quilting as desired. On the sample, in addition to the quilting I did in the appliqué process, I echo quilted around the appliqué design. Refer to "Choosing a Quilting Method" on page 27 for additional guidance as needed.

Making the Block into a Pillow

Refer to "Making the Block into a Pillow" on pages 54–55. Follow steps 1 through 8 to assemble a pillow using the quilted Plaited Pillow block, the two 14" x 10" backing pieces, and the 14" pillow form.

Interpreting Celtic Designs in Hand-Dyed Fabric
"Evening Star" by Beth Ann Williams, Grand Rapids, Michigan, 1999, 36⅝" x 43⅝". A recurring theme in my work is the Celtic concept of "the time between times"—that twilight that is neither day nor night. The wonderful hand-dyed background panel in this wall hanging was prepared especially for me by my friend Lori Verbrugge, owner of the Grand Quilt Company (see "Resources" on page 95). Collection of Verlyn and Lori J. Verbrugge.

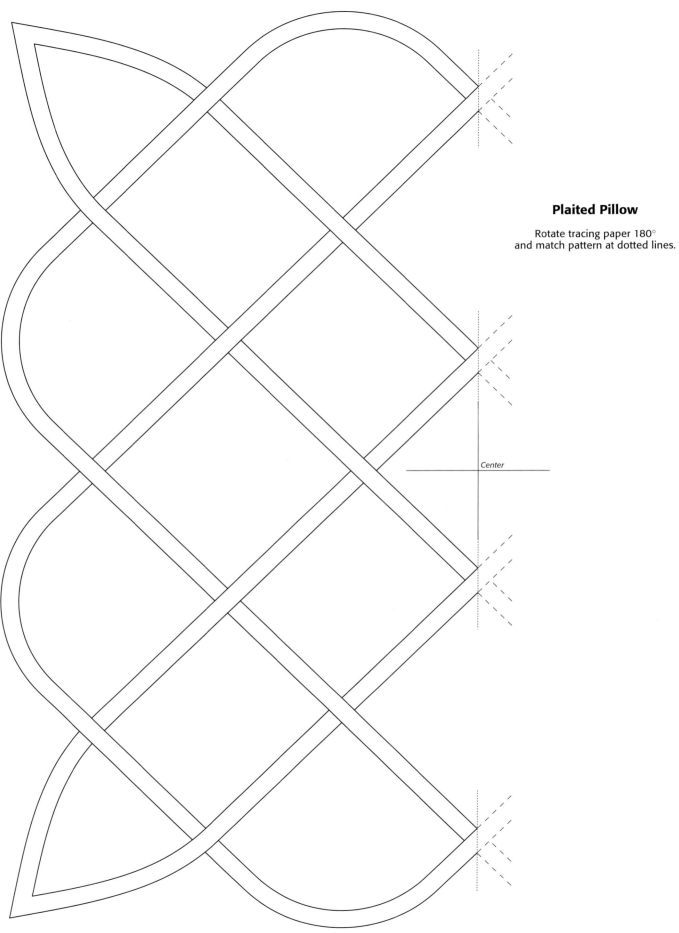

Plaited Pillow

Rotate tracing paper 180°
and match pattern at dotted lines.

Center

Morning Glory

Finished Size: 21½" x 38½"

*T*his modern design was inspired by knotwork and interlace from
ancient Celtic gospel manuscripts. I made this piece as a table
runner, but it is equally suited to hang vertically in an entryway or
horizontally above a couch or bed.

Materials: 42"-wide fabric

½ yd. light fabric for background
⅛ yd. fabric for appliqué insets*
1 fat quarter green fabric for appliqué (bias tubes)
1 fat quarter purple fabric for appliqué (bias tubes)
½ yd. orange fabric for appliqué (bias tubes)
¼ yd. purple mottled print for inner border
¼ yd. contrasting print for accent "flap" border
⅜ yd. multicolored print for outer border
1⅜ yds. fabric for backing
⅜ yd. fabric for binding
24" x 41" piece of low-loft batting
Large sheet (14" x 31" minimum) of tracing paper
Fusible product
* May require ¼ yd. if directional fabric is used.

Cutting

All measurements include ¼"-wide seam allowances.

From the light fabric, cut:
    1 piece, 14" x 32", for appliqué background
From the purple mottled print, cut:
    2 strips, each 2" x 32", for long inner borders
    2 strips, each 2" x 17", for short inner borders
From the contrasting print, cut:
    2 strips, each 1¼" x 35", for long accent "flap" borders
    2 strips, each 1¼" x 17", for short accent "flap" borders
From the multicolored print, cut:
    2 strips, each 2⅞" x 34", for long outer borders
    2 strips, each 2⅞" x 21¾", for short outer borders
From the backing fabric, cut:
    1 piece, 26" x 44", for backing
From the binding fabric, cut:
    4 strips, each 2½" x 42", for binding

Preparing for Appliqué

Refer to "Basic Steps in Creating Celtic-Style Appliqué" on pages 11–35 for general preparation and stitching techniques. Since this is a moderately small project, it is a good opportunity to experiment with appliquéing and quilting in one step. The following instructions are written for that method of construction. If, however, you prefer to appliqué the design onto the quilt top only, then layer and quilt in the traditional manner, please feel free to do so (see "Appliquéing the Design" on pages 21–24 for specifics regarding differences in technique). In other words, choose the method most comfortable to you!

1. Fold and press the 14" x 32" background piece to set the guide marks for centering the appliqué pattern as described in "Preparing the Background Fabric" on page 12.

2. Fold a 14" x 32" piece of tracing paper in the same manner as the background fabric. Align the center marking of pattern section 1 (upper and lower) on pages 69–70 with the center intersections, and the dashed lines with the fold lines on the left-hand side of the tracing paper. Trace sections 1 (upper and lower) and then 2 (page 71) onto the left-hand side of the paper, joining them as indicated. Turn the tracing paper *top to bottom*, once again aligning the center marking on the pattern with the fold lines on the paper. Trace sections 3 and 4, joining the sections at the dashed lines. If you turn the tracing paper in this manner, the "unders" and "overs" of the design flow correctly.

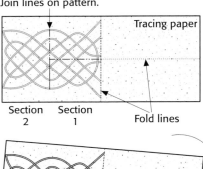

Join lines on pattern.
Tracing paper
Fold lines

Section 2   Section 1

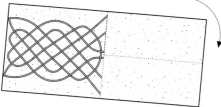

Rotate paper 180°.

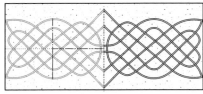

Section 4   Section 3

Finish tracing pattern.

3. Using the guide marks to center the design, transfer the traced pattern to the 14" x 31" background fabric (see "Transferring the Pattern to Fabric" on page 13).

4. Refer to "Placing the Fabric Insets" on page 13. Refer to the placement diagram at right and use your pattern to prepare the insets for bonding. Trace inset pieces A–C onto your preferred fusible. Don't forget to add seam allowances.

   From the inset fabric, cut 4 of A, 4 of B, and 1 of C.

5. Beginning with the outermost insets, bond the insets to the design you have marked on the background fabric, using the placement diagram below and the color photo on page 65 for guidance.

6. Referring to the placement diagram and the color photo, determine the total number of bias strips *of each color* required for this project (see "Preparing the Bias Tubes" on page 14). Use the fat quarters of green and purple fabric and the ½ yard of orange fabric to cut the required number of strips. Cut strips either 1" or 1¼" wide depending upon the method (and foot attachment) you will be using to construct the fabric tubes. Sew and press the fabric tubes.

7. Refer to "'Basting' the Appliqué Design" on page 18 to select the fusing method of your choice. I recommend using Steam-A-Seam2 for this project, although you may choose an alternative method if you wish.

8. Bond the bias tubes in place over the design you have marked on the background fabric.

Placement Diagram

Adding the Borders

Refer to "Adding Borders" on page 24 for detailed instruction as needed.

1. Refer to "Butted (or Squared) Borders" on page 24. With right sides together, pin a 2" x 31" inner border strip to the long sides of the appliquéd panel, aligning the long raw edges. Sew the border strips to the panel using a ¼"-wide seam allowance. Press the seams toward the border strips.

2. Repeat to add the 2" x 17" inner border strips to the short sides of the panel. Press.

3. Refer to "Narrow Accent or 'Flap' Borders" on page 25. Sew a 1¼" x 34" accent border strip to the long sides of the panel to create "flap" borders. Repeat to sew the 1¼" x 17" accent border strips to the short sides of the panel.

4. Sew the 2⅞" x 34" outer borders and the 2⅞" x 21¾" outer borders to the appropriate sides of the quilt as directed in "Narrow Accent or 'Flap' Borders," step 6, on page 25. Press as directed. In this project, I left the flap free, for a three-dimensional accent.

Appliquéing and Quilting in One Step

1. Refer to "Basting the Quilt Sandwich" on page 26. Use your preferred method to layer and baste the quilt top, batting, and backing. Since this is a moderately small project, you may wish to use a quilt basting spray rather than one of the more traditional methods.

2. Stitching through all layers of the quilt sandwich, appliqué the bias tubes. Use nylon monofilament thread and an "invisible" appliqué stitch.

3. Add additional quilting as desired. On the sample, in addition to the quilting I did in the appliqué process, I echo quilted around the appliqué design, quilted in the ditch in the borders, and stipple quilted the balance of the appliqué background. Refer to "Choosing a Quilting Method" on page 27 for additional guidance as needed.

Finishing

1. Trim the batting and backing even with the edges of the quilt top. Square up the quilt as necessary.

2. Use the 2½" x 42" strips to make binding. Bind the quilt to finish.

3. Sign or make a label for your finished quilt.

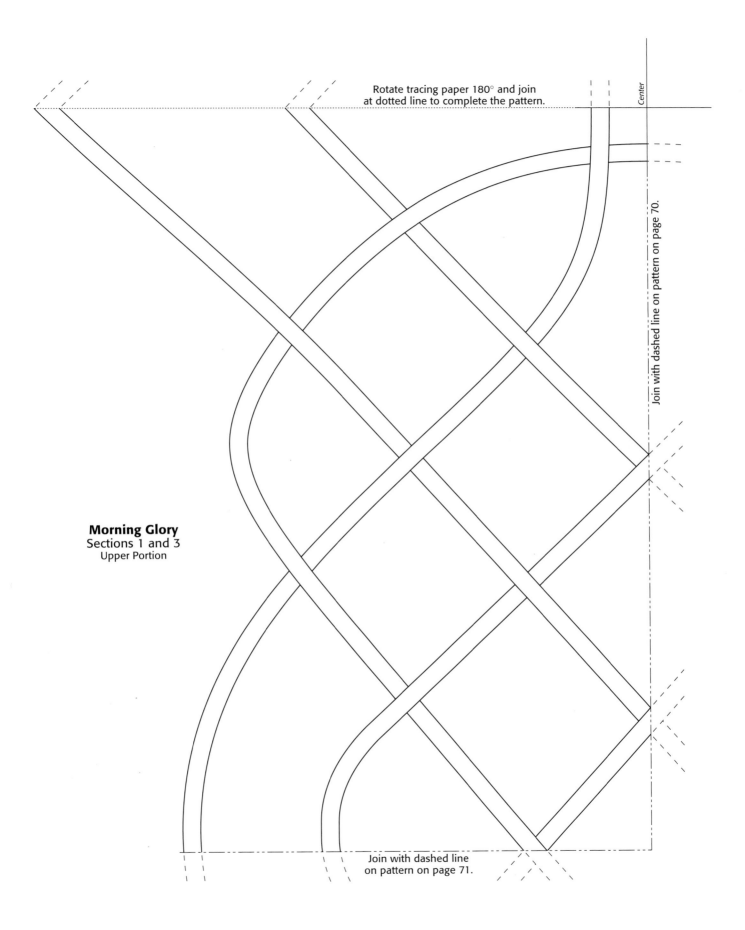

Rotate tracing paper 180° and join
at dotted line to complete the pattern.

Center

Join with dashed line on pattern on page 70.

Morning Glory
Sections 1 and 3
Upper Portion

Join with dashed line
on pattern on page 71.

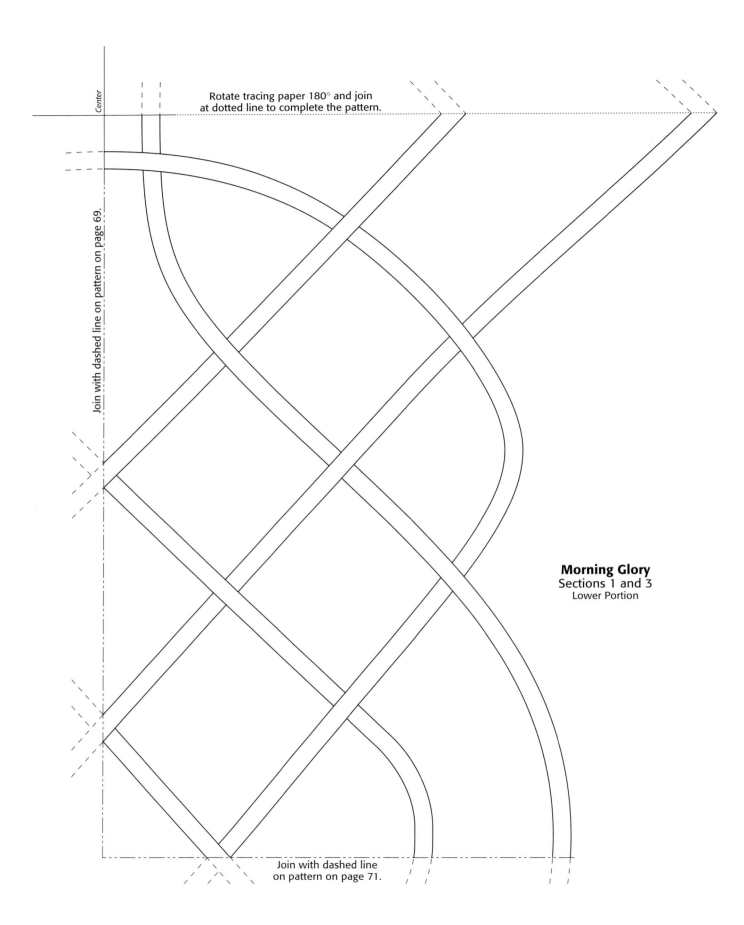

Rotate tracing paper 180° and join at dotted line to complete the pattern.

Center

Join with dashed line on pattern on page 69.

Morning Glory
Sections 1 and 3
Lower Portion

Join with dashed line on pattern on page 71.

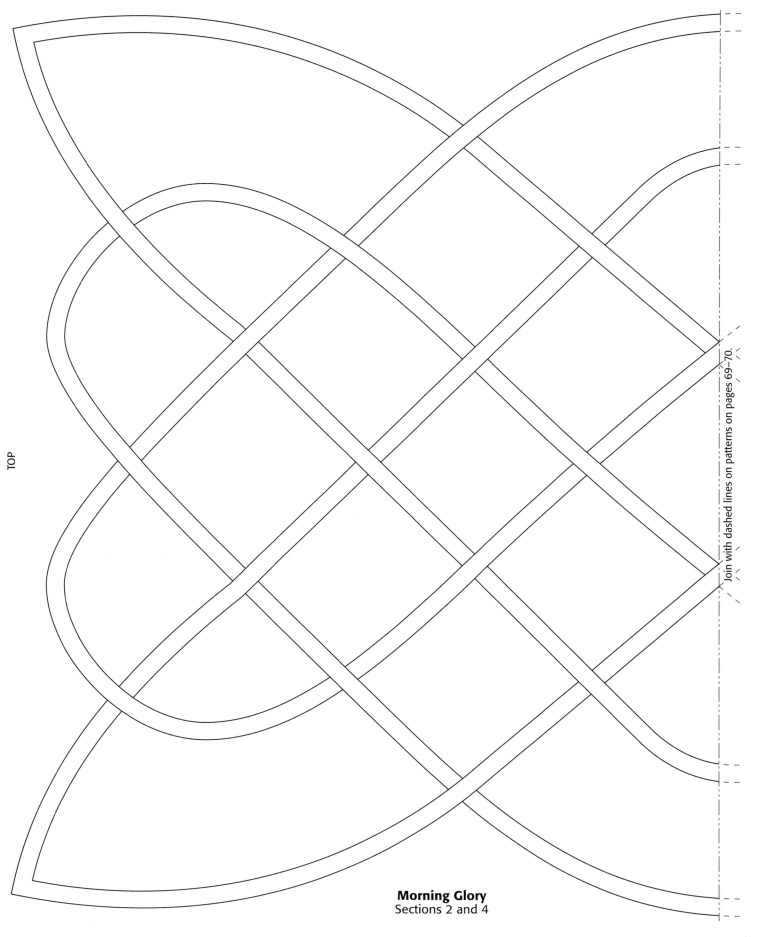

TOP

Join with dashed lines on patterns on pages 69–70.

Morning Glory
Sections 2 and 4

A Celtic Celebration

This versatile design adapts beautifully for a variety of uses, depending upon your choice of fabric. Reds, greens, and golds create a dramatic holiday wall hanging; soft pastels, an heirloom baby quilt; cool blues and silvery whites, a dazzling seasonal snowflake banner. For this project, I recommend the single-surface appliqué method; that is, you complete the appliqué before you layer and quilt the quilt.

Materials: 42"-wide fabric

⅞ yd. light fabric for background

⅛ yd. *each* of 3 constrasting fabrics for appliqué insets

1 fat quarter *each* of 4 contrasting fabrics for appliqué (bias tubes)*

⅓ yd. subtle print for inner border

⅝ yd. multicolored print for outer border

1⅝ yds. fabric for backing and sleeve

½ yd. fabric for binding

42" x 46" piece of low-loft batting

Large sheet (27" x 31" minimum) of tracing paper

Fusible product

*I used gold, dark green, light green, and red.

Cutting

All measurements include ¼"-wide seam allowances.

From the light fabric, cut:

    1 piece, 27" x 31", for background

From the subtle print, cut:

    2 strips, each 2" x 31", for side inner borders

    2 strips, each 2" x 30", for top and bottom inner borders

From the multicolored print, cut:

    2 strips, each 5" x 34", for side outer borders

    2 strips, each 5" x 39", for top and bottom outer borders

From the backing fabric, cut:

    1 piece, 42" x 46", for backing

    1 strip, 9" x 38", for sleeve

From the binding fabric, cut:

    5 strips, each 2½" x 42", for binding

Preparing for Appliqué

Refer to "Basic Steps in Creating Celtic-Style Appliqué" on pages 11–35 for general preparation and stitching techniques.

1. Fold and press the 27" x 31" background piece to set the guide marks for centering the appliqué pattern as described in "Preparing the Background Fabric" on page 12.

2. Fold a 27" x 31" piece of tracing paper in the same manner as the background fabric. Use a yardstick and pencil to mark 2 diagonal lines radiating at 60-degree angles from the center lines as shown.

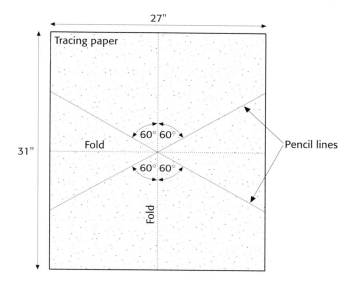

3. Align the center marking of the pattern on page 76 with the vertical fold lines and the marked 60-degree lines on the tracing paper. Refer to the placement diagram on page 74 for guidance as necessary. Trace the pattern onto the paper.

4. In a similar fashion, align the center marking of the corner pattern on page 75 with the vertical fold lines and the marked 60-degree lines on the tracing paper. Refer to the placement diagram on page 75 for guidance. Trace the pattern onto the paper.

5. Using the guide marks to center the design, transfer the traced pattern to the 27" x 31" background piece (see "Transferring the Pattern to Fabric" on page 13).

6. Refer to "Placing the Fabric Insets" on page 13. Refer to the placement diagram and use your pattern to prepare the insets for bonding. Trace inset pieces A–D onto your preferred fusible. Don't forget to add seam allowances.

   From inset fabric #1, cut 6 *each* of A and B. From inset fabric #2, cut 6 of C. From inset fabric #3, cut 1 of D.

7. Beginning with the outermost insets (A), bond the insets to the design you have marked on the background fabric, using the placement diagram and the color photo on page 72 for guidance.

8. Referring to the placement diagram and the color photo, determine the total number of bias strips *of each color* required for this project (see "Preparing the Bias Tubes" on page 14). Use the fat quarters of contrasting fabrics to cut the required number of strips. Strips will be cut either 1" or 1¼" wide depending upon the method (and foot attachment) you will be using to construct the fabric tubes. Sew and press the fabric tubes.

9. Refer to "'Basting' the Appliqué Design" on page 18 to select the fusing method of your choice. I recommend using Steam-A-Seam2 for this project, although you may choose an alternative method if you wish.

10. Bond the bias tubes in place over the design you have marked on the background fabric.

Single-Surface Appliqué

Referring to "Appliquéing the Design" on pages 21–24, appliqué the bias tubes to the background block. Use nylon monofilament thread and an "invisible" appliqué stitch.

Placement Diagram

Adding the Borders

Refer to "Butted (or Squared) Borders" on page 24 for detailed instruction as needed.

1. With right sides together, pin a 2" x 31" inner border strip to both the left and right sides of the appliquéd block, aligning the long raw edges. Sew the border strips to the block, using a ¼"-wide seam. Press the seams toward the border strips.
2. Repeat to add the 2" x 30" inner border strips to the top and bottom edges of the block. Press.
3. In the same fashion, add the 5" x 34" side and the 5" x 39" top and bottom outer borders to the appropriate sides of the quilt.

Layering and Quilting

1. Refer to "Basting the Quilt Sandwich" on page 26. Use your preferred method to layer and baste the quilt top, batting, and backing. Since this is a somewhat larger project, you may wish to baste the quilt sandwich with safety pins.
2. Quilt as desired. On the sample, I quilted in the ditch and echo quilted around the appliqué design and in the borders. I added spirals in the inner border, channel quilted the outer border, and stipple quilted the balance of the appliqué background. Refer to "Choosing a Quilting Method" on page 27 for additional guidance as needed.

Finishing

1. Trim the batting and backing even with the edges of the quilt top. Square up the quilt as necessary.
2. Use the 9" x 38" strip of backing fabric to construct and sew a hanging sleeve to the back of the quilt sandwich.
3. Use the 2½" x 42" strips to make binding. Bind the quilt to finish.
4. Sign or make a label for your finished quilt.

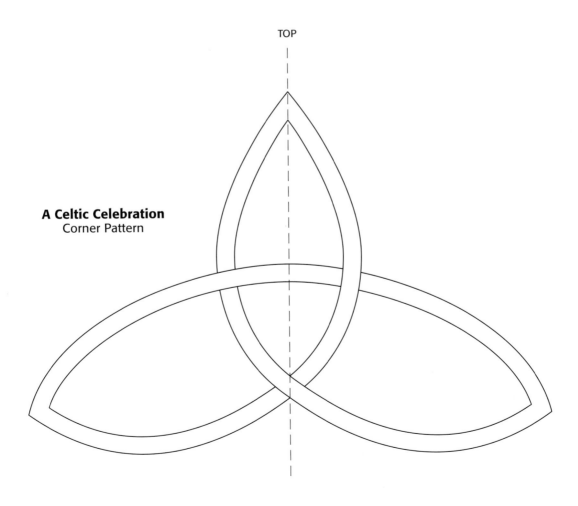

A Celtic Celebration
Corner Pattern

TOP

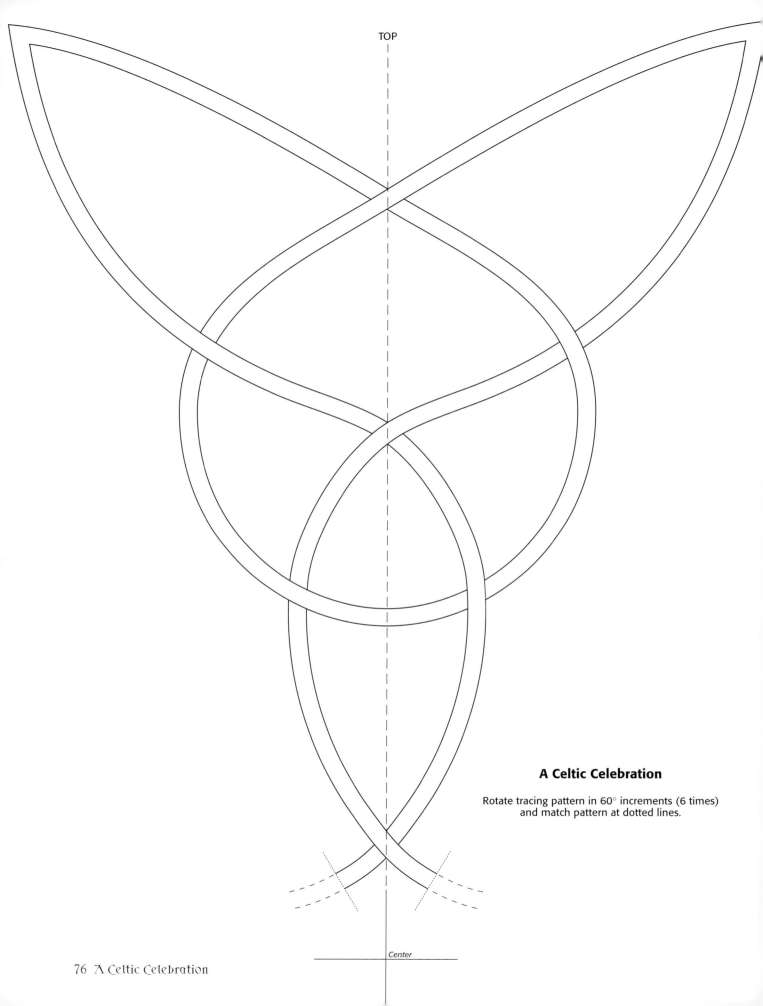

TOP

A Celtic Celebration

Rotate tracing pattern in 60° increments (6 times)
and match pattern at dotted lines.

Center

Wheel Around the Sun

Finished Size: 19" x 19"

I stitched up this pattern as a table mat to coordinate with "A Celtic Celebration" on page 72. I use it with a chunky brass pillar-candle holder that looks great in the center! It also works well, with or without the insets, as a wall hanging on its own, as a large pillow, or as a large repeat block for a bed-size quilt.

Materials: 42"-wide fabric

⅜ yd. light fabric for background
⅛ yd. subtle print for appliqué insets*
½ yd. contrasting fabric for appliqué (bias tubes)
⅔ yd. fabric for backing
¼ yd. fabric for binding
21" x 21" square of low-loft batting
Large sheet (19" x 19" minimum) of tracing paper
Fusible product
*Directional fabric requires ¼ yard.

Cutting

*All measurements include ¼"-wide
seam allowances.*

From the light fabric, cut:
  1 square, 19" x 19", for background
From the backing fabric, cut:
  1 square, 22" x 22", for backing
From the binding fabric, cut:
  3 strips, each 2½" x 42", for binding

Preparing for Appliqué

Refer to "Basic Steps in Creating Celtic-Style Appliqué" on pages 11–35 for general preparation and stitching techniques. Since this is a small project, it is a good opportunity to experiment with appliquéing and quilting in one step. The following instructions are written for that method of construction. If, however, you prefer to appliqué the design onto the quilt top only, then layer and quilt in the traditional manner, please feel free to do so (see "Appliquéing the Design" on pages 21–24 for specifics regarding differences in technique). In other words, choose the method most comfortable to you!

1. Fold and press the 19" square of background fabric to set the guide marks for centering the appliqué pattern as described in "Preparing the Background Fabric" on page 12. Fold the fabric again from corner to corner in both directions to mark diagonals.

2. Fold a 19" square of tracing paper in the same manner as the background fabric. Align the center marking of the pattern on page 80 with the fold lines on the tracing paper. Trace the pattern onto the paper. Turn the tracing paper as directed and trace the rest of the pattern, carefully aligning the center marking and registration lines and joining the sections at the dotted lines as indicated. If you turn the tracing paper in this manner, the "unders" and "overs" of the design will flow correctly.

3. Using the guide marks to center the design, transfer the traced pattern to the 19" square of background fabric (see "Transferring the Pattern to Fabric" on page 13).

4. Refer to "Placing the Fabric Insets" on page 13. Referring to the placement diagram below, use your pattern to prepare the insets for bonding. Trace inset piece A onto your preferred fusible. Don't forget to add seam allowances.

From the inset fabric, cut 7 of A.

Placement Diagram

5. Bond the insets to the design you have marked on the background fabric, using the placement diagram and the color photo on page 77 for guidance.

6. Determine the total number of bias strips required for this project (see "Preparing the Bias Tubes" on page 14). Use the ½ yard of contrasting fabric to cut the required number of strips. Strips will be cut either 1" or 1¼"

wide depending upon the method (and foot attachment) you will be using to construct the fabric tubes. Sew and press the fabric tubes.

7. Refer to " 'Basting' the Appliqué Design" on page 18 to select the fusing method of your choice. I recommend using Steam-A-Seam2 for this project, although you may choose an alternative method if you wish.

8. Bond the bias tubes in place over the design you have marked on the background fabric.

Appliquéing and Quilting in One Step

1. Refer to "Basting the Quilt Sandwich" on page 26. Use your preferred method to layer and baste the quilt top, batting, and backing. Since this is a small project, you may wish to use a quilt basting spray rather than one of the more traditional methods.

2. Stitching through all layers of the quilt sandwich, appliqué the bias tubes. Use nylon monofilament thread and an "invisible" appliqué stitch.

3. Add additional quilting as desired. On the sample, in addition to the quilting I did in the appliqué process, I echo quilted around the appliqué design and stipple quilted the balance of the appliqué background. Refer to "Choosing a Quilting Method" on page 27 for additional guidance as needed.

Finishing

1. Trim the batting and backing even with the edges of the quilt top. Square up the quilt top as necessary.

2. Use the 2½" x 42" strips to make binding. Bind the quilt to finish.

3. Sign or make a label for your finished quilt.

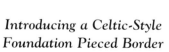

Introducing a Celtic-Style Foundation Pieced Border
"In Memoriam" by Beth Ann Williams, 1995, Grand Rapids, Michigan, 37½" x 37½". A classic Celtic Greek key pattern borders an impressionistic cross. Metallic thread is used to superimpose a Celtic knot on the cross and to give the surrounding area a subtle glow. Made as a memorial piece for a cherished friend. Collection of Dr. James King.

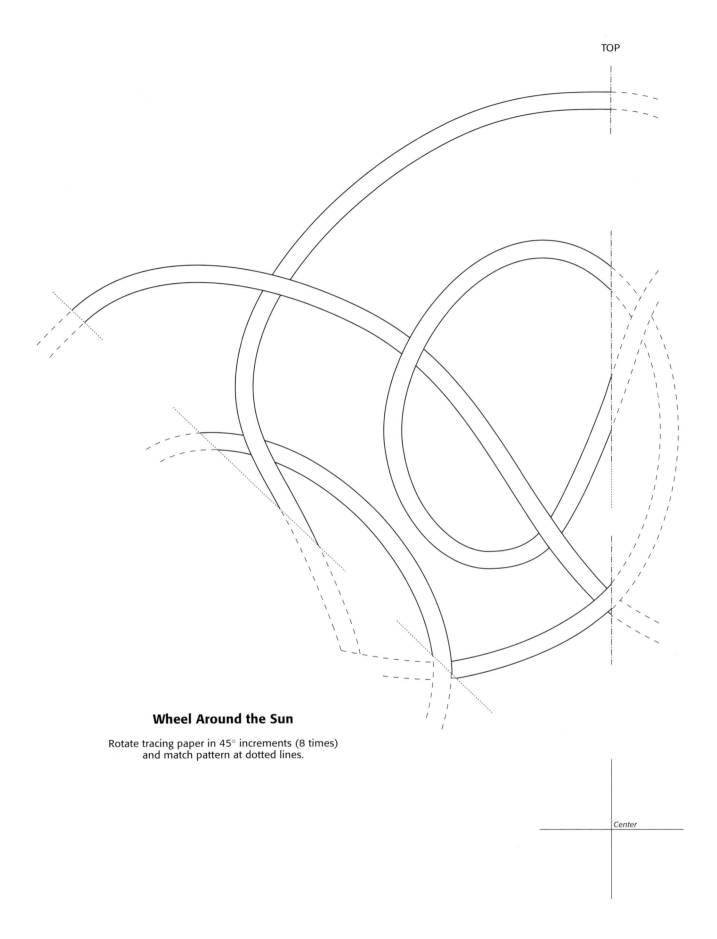

TOP

Wheel Around the Sun

Rotate tracing paper in 45° increments (8 times)
and match pattern at dotted lines.

Center

Ode to King Cormac

Finished Size: 47½" x 56"

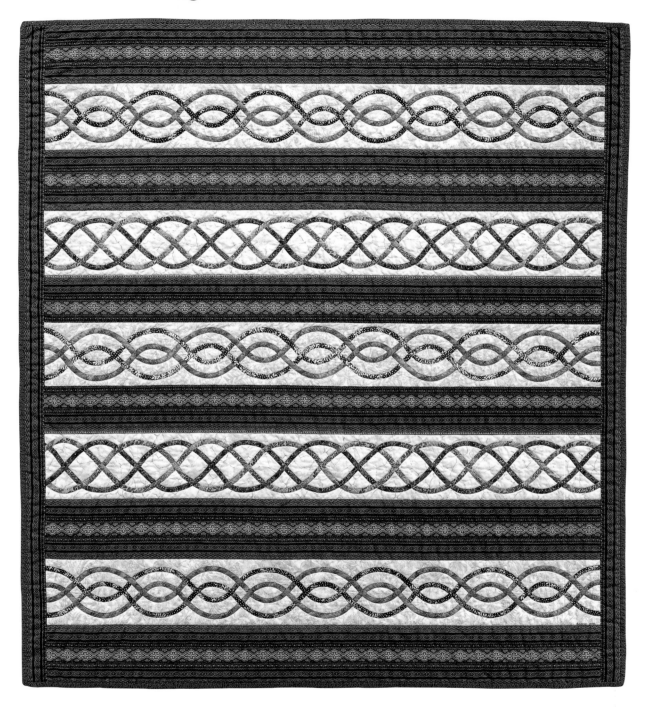

*T*his project is sized to drape over the back of a couch or large easy chair. It was inspired by ancient Celtic war helmets decorated with rows of interlace and by traditional strippy quilts. To adapt the pattern for a bed quilt, make the appliquéd panels as long as required to run vertically down the bed. For this project, I recommend the single-surface appliqué method. Appliqué each panel separately before joining them together; then baste and quilt the quilt top.

Materials: 42"-wide fabric

1⅓ yds. light fabric for background A*

1⅓ yds. light fabric for background B*

1⅝ yds. dark border stripe for sashing and side borders**

½ yd. *each* of 5 different medium and/or dark fabrics for applique (bias tubes)

3 yds. fabric for backing

½ yd. fabric for binding

Fusible product

50" x 58" piece of low-loft batting

*If you prefer, you can use the same background fabric for all 5 appliquéd strips, which requires 1⅓ yds. *total* light fabric.

**May require additional yardage depending upon border repeat.

Cutting

All measurements include ¼"-wide seam allowances.

NOTE: *With the exception of the binding, cut all strips for this project on the* lengthwise *(parallel to the selvage) straight of grain.*

From light fabric A, cut:
  3 strips, each 6" x 44", for background A*

From light fabric B, cut:
  2 strips, each 6" x 44", for background B*

From the dark border stripe, cut:
  4 strips, each 5½" x 44", for sashing
  2 strips, each 4½" x 44", for sashing
  2 strips, each 2¼" x 56", for side borders

From the binding fabric, cut:
  6 strips, each 2½" x 42", for binding

*OR cut 5 strips, each 6" x 44", from a single light fabric

Preparing the Appliqué

Refer to "Basic Steps in Creating Celtic-Style Appliqué" on pages 11–35 for general preparation and stitching techniques. You will need three panels of appliqué design A to stitch to background fabric A, and two panels of appliqué design B to stitch to background fabric B.

1. Fold and press each 6" x 44" background panel to set the guide marks as described in "Preparing the Background Fabric" on page 12.

2. Use the pattern on page 85 to transfer appliqué design A to each of the three 6" x 44" Fabric A panels. Begin marking in the center of each strip, aligning the center marking on the pattern with the fold lines on the fabric. Continue marking the design outward from the center point in both directions, joining the pattern at the dotted lines as indicated. Keep the center marking on the pattern aligned with the long fold line on the fabric. This helps you to keep the marked design lined up perfectly down the panel's center.

TIP

By marking the appliqué design outward from the center of each background panel, you'll ensure that the design begins and ends in the same spot as it reaches the panel's outer edges.

3. Repeat the process described in step 2 to transfer appliqué design B (page 86) to each of the two 6" x 44" Fabric B background panels.

4. Referring to the placement diagram on page 83 and the color photo on page 81, determine the total number of bias strips *of each color* required for this project (see "Preparing the Bias Tubes" on page 14). Use the ½-yard pieces of medium and/or dark fabrics to cut

the required number of strips. Strips will be cut either 1" or 1¼" wide depending upon the method (and foot attachment) you will be using to construct the fabric tubes. Sew and press the fabric tubes.

NOTE: *Two panels of appliqué design A combine strips of appliqué fabrics #1 and #2, one panel of appliqué design A combines strips of appliqué fabrics #1 and #5, and both panels of appliqué design B combine appliqué fabrics # 3 and #4.*

Appliqué Pattern A
Make 2.

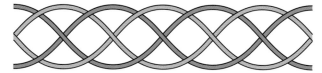

Appliqué Pattern B
Make 2.

Appliqué Pattern A
Make 1.

Placement Diagrams

Fabric #1   Fabric #2   Fabric #3
Fabric #4   Fabric #5

5. Refer to " 'Basting' the Appliqué Design" on page 18 to select the fusing method of your choice. I recommend using Steam-A-Seam2 for this project, although you may choose an alternative method if you wish.

6. Bond the bias tubes in place over the designs you have marked on the background panels.

Single-Surface Appliqué

Referring to "Appliquéing the Design" on pages 21–24, appliqué the appropriate bias tubes to each background panel. Refer to the placement diagram at left and the color photo on page 81 for guidance. Use nylon monofilament thread and an "invisible" appliqué stitch.

Assembling the Quilt Top

1. Refer to the quilt diagram below. Use a design wall or other large, flat surface to lay out alternating rows of appliqué panels and sashing strips as shown. Note that the sashing strips framing the center panel are the narrower (4½"-wide) strips.

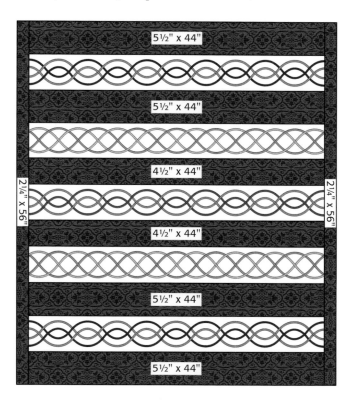

Quilt Diagram
Note: Border measurements are cut measurements.

2. With right sides together and long raw edges aligned, pin and sew the sashings and panels together. Press the seam allowances away from the appliquéd strips.

3. With right sides together and long raw edges aligned, pin and sew a 2¼" x 56" border strip to opposite sides of the quilt top. Press the seams toward the border strips. Refer to "Adding Borders" on page 24 for guidance if necessary.

Layering and Quilting

1. Remove the selvages and divide the backing fabric into two 42" x 54" pieces. With right sides together, sew the pieces together along one long raw edge to make a single large backing panel.

2. Refer to "Basting the Quilt Sandwich" on page 26. Use your preferred method to layer and baste the quilt top, batting, and backing. Since this is a somewhat large project, you may wish to baste the quilt sandwich with safety pins.

3. Quilt as desired. On the sample, I quilted in the ditch and echo quilted around the appliqué design and in the sashing and borders. Then I channel quilted the sashing and borders as well. Refer to "Choosing a Quilting Method" on page 27 for additional guidance as needed.

Finishing

1. Trim the batting and backing even with the edges of the quilt top. Square up the quilt as necessary.

2. Use the 2½" x 42" strips to make binding. Bind the quilt to finish.

3. Sign or make a label for your finished quilt.

Combining Celtic Motifs and Jacobean Appliqué

"Tree of Life" by Beth Ann Williams, 1999, Grand Rapids, Michigan, 36" x 39½". The Tree of Life is a deeply powerful recurring symbol in many cultures. The Jacobean appliqué in the center of this wall hanging was adapted from patterns published by Mimi Ayars, Ph.D., and Patricia B. Campbell in their book Jacobean Applique: Book 2— "Romantica" Vol 1. The motifs are derived from floral and arboreal embroideries characteristic of the period named for King James I (James VI of Scotland). Formally known as "Jacobus Britanniae Rex," James was the successor to Queen Elizabeth I, and united the thrones of Scotland and England in 1603.

The Celtic-style interlaced border is woven of one continuous strand. It never ends, but continues to weave over and under itself as it flows around the tree.

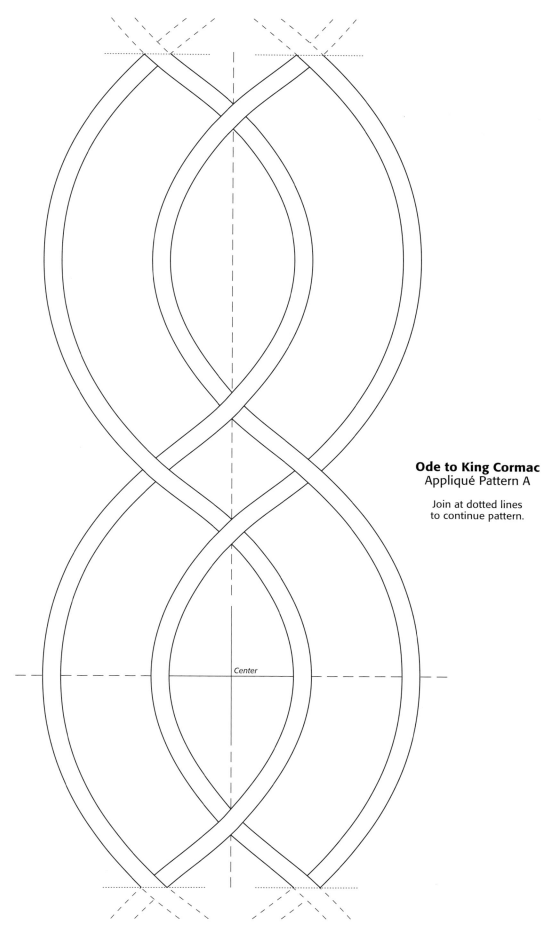

Ode to King Cormac
Appliqué Pattern A

Join at dotted lines
to continue pattern.

Center

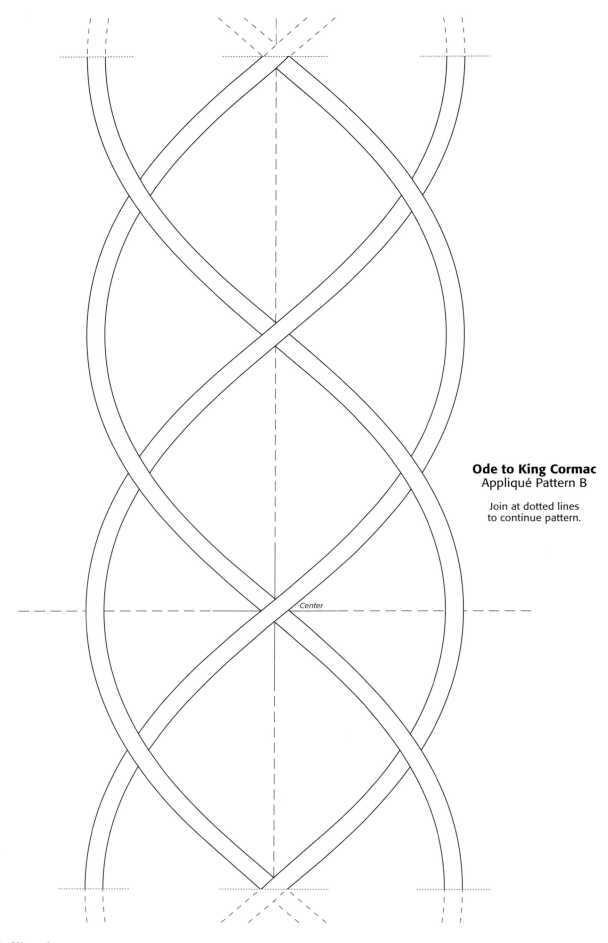

Ode to King Cormac
Appliqué Pattern B

Join at dotted lines
to continue pattern.

Center

The Island

*T*he colors and rhythms of this quilt were inspired by a poignant lament attributed to Colmcille, also known as St. Columba, a warrior Celt of noble birth who could have been by right a king, but chose to become a monk instead. This lament was written in the sixth century A.D. while Colmcille was in exile, and is full of images of his beloved homeland. For this project, I recommend the single-surface appliqué method.

Materials: 42"-wide fabric

1 yd. light fabric for background
1¼ yds. medium-dark print for outer border and
    appliqué insets (center medallion)
¼ yd. light-medium fabric for appliqué insets
    (center medallion)
¼ yd. dark fabric for appliqué insets (border)
½ yd. *each* of 2 contrasting fabrics for appliqué
    (bias tubes in center medallion and border)
1 fat quarter fabric for appliqué (bias tubes in
    center medallion)
1⅝ yds. fabric for backing and sleeve
⅜ yd. fabric for binding
38" x 43" piece of low-loft batting
Large sheet (33" x 37" minimum) of tracing
    paper
Fusible product

Cutting

*All measurements include ¼"-wide
seam allowances.*

From the light fabric, cut:
    1 piece, 33" x 37", for appliqué background
From the medium-dark print, cut:
    1 piece, 36" x 40½", for outer border
From the backing fabric, cut:
    1 piece, 42" x 46", for backing
    1 strip, 9" x 36", for sleeve
From the binding fabric, cut:
    4 strips, each 2½" x 42", for binding

Transferring the Pattern

Refer to "Basic Steps in Creating Celtic-Style Appliqué" on pages 11–35 for general preparation techniques. You will be marking the entire design (center medallion and border appliqué) on the background fabric.

1. Fold and press the 33" x 37" background piece to set the guide marks for centering the appliqué pattern as described in "Preparing the Background Fabric" on page 12.

2. Fold a 33" x 37" piece of tracing paper in the same manner as the background fabric. On a photocopy machine, enlarge the patterns on pages 92–94 by 200 percent. Position the enlarged pattern from page 92 under the upper-left quadrant of the tracing paper, aligning the center marking of the pattern with the fold lines on the paper. Trace the pattern onto the paper.

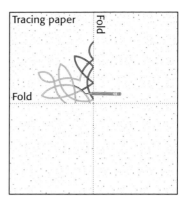

3. Turn the tracing paper *top to bottom*, once again aligning the center marking on the pattern with the fold lines on the paper. Trace the pattern onto the lower-right quadrant of the paper.

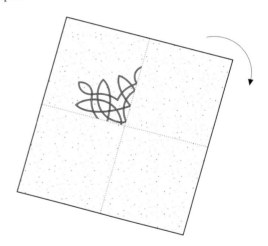

Turn tracing paper top to bottom.

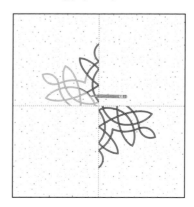

4. In a similar fashion, trace the enlarged pattern from page 94 onto the upper-right and lower-left quadrants of the paper. Join the new sections with the previously traced sections at the dashed lines on the pattern.

5. To transfer the border, align the center marking of the enlarged pattern from page 93 with the fold line along the top edge of the tracing paper. Trace the design onto the paper, approximately 1⅜" from the outer edge. Repeat for the bottom edge. In the same manner, use the enlarged pattern from page 94 to trace the two side border segments onto the tracing paper, approximately 2⅜" from the outer edge.

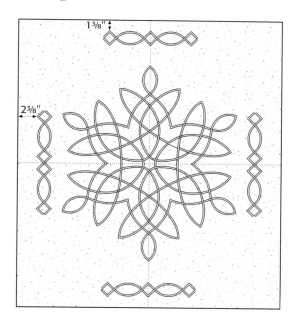

6. Use the enlarged patterns from pages 92 and 94 to trace and complete each corner of the border design. Join the corners with the previously traced sections at the dashed lines marked on the patterns. Refer to the placement diagram on page 91 and the color photo on page 87 for guidance as necessary.

7. Using the guide marks to center the diagram, transfer the traced pattern to the 33" x 37" background piece (see "Transferring the Pattern to Fabric" on page 13).

Preparing the Appliqué

Refer to "Basic Steps in Creating Celtic-Style Appliqué" on pages 11–35 for general preparation and stitching techniques.

1. Refer to "Placing the Fabric Insets" on page 13. Use your enlarged, full-size pattern to prepare the insets for bonding. Trace inset pieces A–D onto your preferred fusible. Don't forget to add seam allowances.

   From the remaining medium-dark print, cut 6 of A and 1 of C. From the light-medium inset fabric, cut 6 of B. From the dark inset fabric, cut 18 of D. Set the D insets aside for now.

2. Bond insets A–C to the center medallion appliqué design you have marked on the background fabric, using the placement diagram and the color photo for guidance.

3. Referring to the placement diagram and the color photo, determine the total number of bias strips *of each color* required for this project (see "Preparing the Bias Tubes" on page 14). Use the three bias tube fabrics to cut the required number of strips. Strips will be cut either 1" or 1¼" wide depending upon the method (and foot attachment) you will be using to construct the fabric tubes. Sew and press the fabric tubes. Set the tubes to be used for the interlace border aside for now.

4. Refer to "'Basting' the Appliqué Design" on page 18 to select the fusing method of your choice. I recommend using Steam-A-Seam2 for this project, although you may choose an alternative method if you wish.

5. Bond the appropriate bias tubes in place over the center medallion appliqué design you have marked on the background fabric.

Appliquéing the Center Medallion

Referring to "Appliquéing the Design" on pages 21–24, appliqué the bias tubes to the background block, using the single-surface technique. Use nylon monofilament thread and an "invisible" appliqué stitch.

Creating the Scalloped Border

Refer to "Basic Steps in Creating Celtic-Style Appliqué" on pages 11–35 for general preparation and stitching techniques.

1. Center and pin the background fabric (with the completed medallion) on the 36" x 40½" piece of border fabric.
2. Sew a single line of stitching *between* the double lines marking the placement of the border bias tubes.

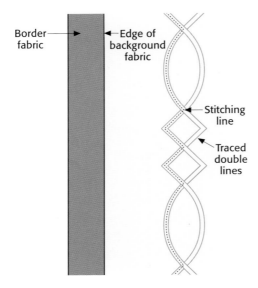

Border fabric

Edge of background fabric

Stitching line

Traced double lines

3. Carefully trim away the excess background fabric *outside the stitched line*, revealing the border fabric underneath. Leave a seam allowance approximately $\frac{3}{16}$" wide.

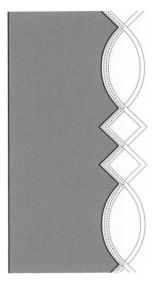

Trim medallion background fabric
³⁄₁₆" from stitching.

4. Turn the quilt top over and trim the border fabric from behind the background fabric, again leaving a $\frac{3}{16}$"-wide seam allowance.

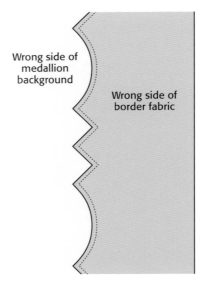

Wrong side of medallion background

Wrong side of border fabric

Trim border fabric
³⁄₁₆" from stitching.

5. Fuse the D insets to the border design you have marked on the background fabric. Use the placement diagram on page 91 and the color photo on page 87 for guidance.

6. Bond the border bias tubes in place, covering all raw edges where the background and border fabrics have been sewn and trimmed (see "'Basting' the Appliqué Design" on page 18). Refer to the placement diagram and color photo as needed.

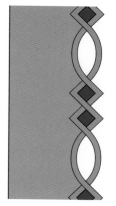

7. Use the single-surface technique to appliqué the interlacing bias tubes to the quilt top.

Layering and Quilting

1. Refer to "Basting the Quilt Sandwich" on page 26. Use your preferred method to layer and baste the quilt top, batting, and backing. Since this is a somewhat large project, you may wish to baste the quilt sandwich with safety pins.

2. Quilt as desired. On the sample, I quilted in the ditch and echo quilted around the appliqué design and the interlaced borders. I stipple quilted the balance of the medallion background and filled the outer border with spirals and crescents. Refer to "Choosing a Quilting Method" on page 27 for additional guidance as needed.

Finishing

1. Trim the batting and backing even with the edges of the quilt top. Square up the quilt as necessary.

2. Use the 9" x 36" strip of backing fabric to construct and sew a hanging sleeve to the back of the quilt sandwich.

3. Use the 2½" x 42" strips to make binding. Bind the quilt to finish.

4. Sign or make a label for your finished quilt.

Placement Diagram

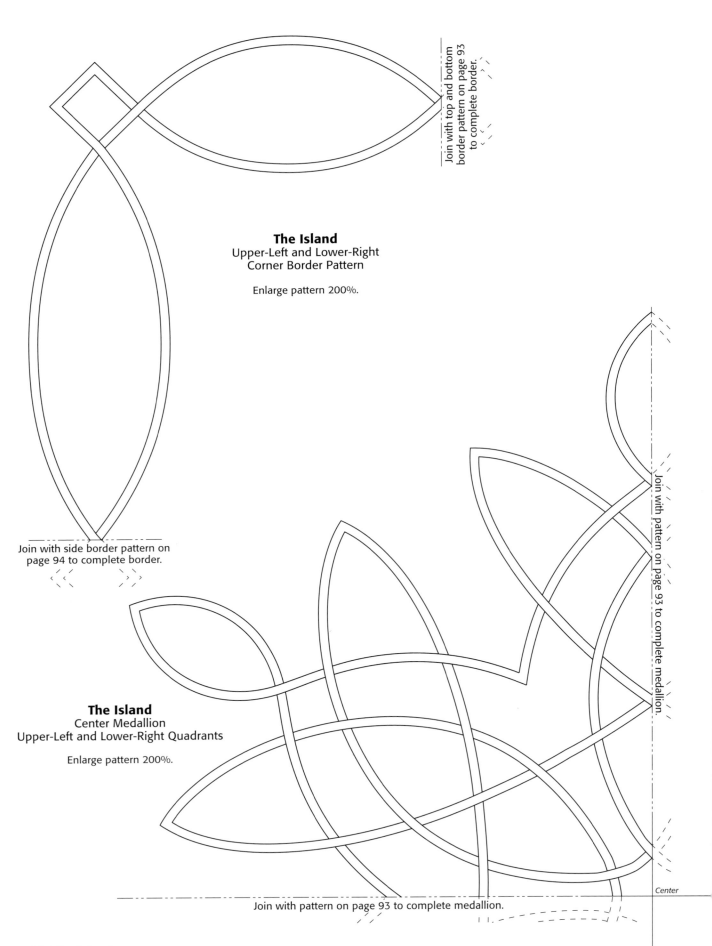

The Island
Upper-Left and Lower-Right
Corner Border Pattern

Enlarge pattern 200%.

Join with top and bottom border pattern on page 93 to complete border.

Join with side border pattern on page 94 to complete border.

Join with pattern on page 93 to complete medallion.

The Island
Center Medallion
Upper-Left and Lower-Right Quadrants

Enlarge pattern 200%.

Join with pattern on page 93 to complete medallion.

Center

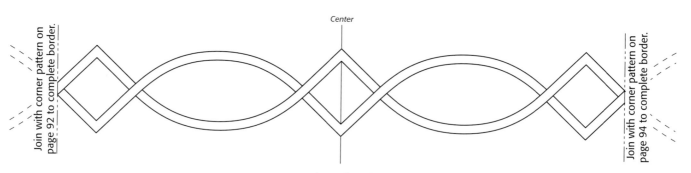

Join with corner pattern on page 92 to complete border.

Center

Join with corner pattern on page 94 to complete border.

The Island
Top and Bottom Border Pattern

Enlarge pattern 200%.

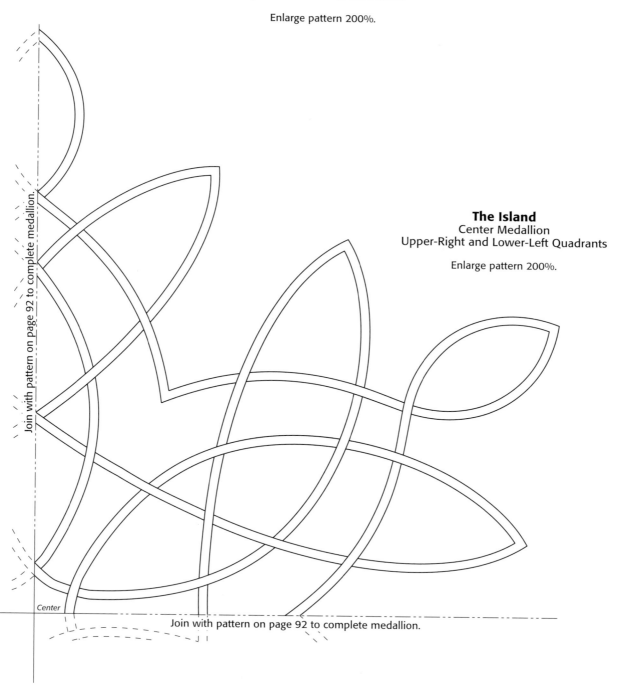

Join with pattern on page 92 to complete medallion.

The Island
Center Medallion
Upper-Right and Lower-Left Quadrants

Enlarge pattern 200%.

Center

Join with pattern on page 92 to complete medallion.

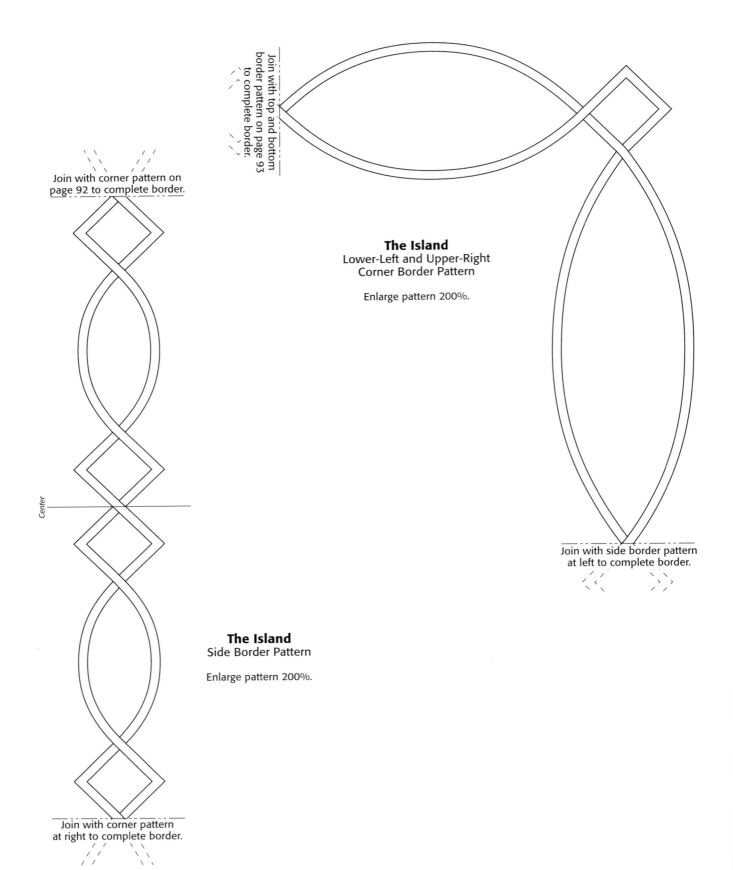

Join with corner pattern on
page 92 to complete border.

Join with top and bottom
border pattern on page 93
to complete border.

The Island
Lower-Left and Upper-Right
Corner Border Pattern

Enlarge pattern 200%.

Join with side border pattern
at left to complete border.

Center

The Island
Side Border Pattern

Enlarge pattern 200%.

Join with corner pattern
at right to complete border.

Bibliography and Suggestions for Further Reading

Quilting Techniques

Campbell, Patricia B. and Mimi Ayars, Ph.D. *Jacobean Appliqué: Book II—"Romantica."* Paducah, Ky.: American Quilter's Society, 1995.

Deitrich, Mimi. *Basic Quiltmaking Techniques for Hand Appliqué.* Bothell, Wash.: That Patchwork Place, 1998.

Hargrave, Harriet. *Heirloom Machine Quilting: A Comprehensive Guide to Hand-Quilted Effects Using Your Sewing Machine.* Lafayette, Calif.: C&T Publishing, 1995.

Hussain, Donna. *Interlacing Borders: More than 100 Intricate Designs Made Easy.* Bothell, Wash.: Martingale & Company, 1998.

Lawther, Gail. *The Complete Quilting Course.* Radnor, Pa.: Chilton Book Company, 1992.

Madden, Angela. *Magic Celtic: Sectional Designing, Speedy Sewing.* Harpenden, Herts, England: M.C.Q. Publications, 1994.

Noble, Maurine. *Machine Quilting Made Easy.* Bothell, Wash.: That Patchwork Place, Inc., 1994.

Osler, Dorothy. *Quilting Design Sourcebook.* Bothell, Wash.: That Patchwork Place, Inc., 1996.

Wiechec, Philomena. *Celtic Quilt Designs.* Sunnyvale, Calif.: Celtic Design Co., 1980.

Celtic Art

Bain, George. *Celtic Art: The Methods of Construction.* New York: Dover Publications, Inc., 1973.

Bain, Ian. *Celtic Knotwork.* New York: Sterling Publishing Co., Inc., 1992.

Davis, Courtney. *Celtic Ornament: Art of the Scribe.* London: Blandford, 1996.

Delaney, Frank. *The Celts.* Great Britain: BBC Publications and Hodder & Stoughton Ltd., 1986.

Green, Miranda. *Celtic Art: Symbols & Imagery.* New York: Sterling Publishing Co., Inc., 1997.

Jacobsthal, Paul. *Early Celtic Art, Vols. I and II.* Oxford University Press, 1944.

Meehan, Aidan. *Knotwork: The Secret Method of the Scribes.* New York: Thames & Hudson, 1991.

Meehan, Bernard. *The Book of Kells: An Illustrated Introduction of the Manuscript in Trinity College Dublin.* London: Thames and Hudson Ltd., 1994.

Megaw, Ruth and Vincent Meegaw. *Celtic Art: From Its Beginnings to the Book of Kells.* New York: Thames & Hudson, Inc., 1990.

Sturrock, Sheila. *Celtic Knotwork Designs.* New York: Sterling Publishing Co., Inc., 1997.

Resources

I purchase some of my supplies from the following companies:

Grand Quilt Company
5290 Alpine Avenue NW
Comstock Park, MI 49321
Phone: (616) 647-1120
Fax: (616) 647-1074
grquiltco@aol.com
www.grandquilt.com

Connecting Threads
PO Box 8940
Vancouver, WA 98668-8940
Phone: (800) 574-6454
Fax: (360) 260-8877
www.ConnectingThreads.com
Free catalog upon request.

Clotilde
Box 3000
Louisiana, MO 63353-3000
Phone: (800) 722-2891 (US)
(573) 754-7979 (outside US)
Fax: (800) 863-3191 (US)
(573) 754-3109 (outside US)
www.clotilde.com
Free catalog upon request.

The Stencil Company
28 Castlewood Drive, Dept. C
Cheektowaga, NY 14227-2615
Phone: (716) 656-9430
Fax: (716) 668-2488
stencil@webt.com
www.quiltingstencils.com
Catalog available for $1.

Nancy's Notions
PO Box 683
Beaver Dam, WI 53916-0683
Order Line: 1-800-833-0690
Fax: 1-800-255-8119
www.nancysnotions.com
Free catalog upon request.

About the Author

Photo by Amy Logsdon

*B*eth Ann Williams is an award-winning quiltmaker, collector, teacher, and designer. Having lived in different countries and on different continents, she has enjoyed a lifetime exposure to the richness of varied cultural and artistic traditions and a particular fascination with textiles. As a fourth-generation quiltmaker (at least!), Beth has a profound respect for the traditional approach to quiltmaking. However, she is probably best known for her contemporary quilts and innovative methods. In addition to Celtic quilt styles, she teaches in a variety of other subject areas, including decorative machine quilting, heirloom machine appliqué, Impressionist-style piecing, bargello quilting, abstract design, and color theory.

Beth holds a B.A. in communication arts from Cedarville College, Cedarville, Ohio. She is a member of the American Quilter's Society, the American Quilt Study Group, the National Quilting Association, and the West Michigan Quilters Guild.

Since 1990, Beth has lived in Grand Rapids, Michigan, with her husband, John, and their two daughters, Caryl and Connor.